Adventures
AT HOME

Adventures
AT HOME

40 Ways to Make Happy Family Memories

Zoë Lake

Pimpernel
Press Ltd
www.pimpernelpress.com

Pimpernel Press Limited
www.pimpernelpress.com

Adventures at Home
© Pimpernel Press Limited 2022
Text and photographs
© Zoë Lake 2022 except for
those listed below.

A catalogue record for this book is
available from the British Library.

ISBN 978-1-914902-99-4

Typeset in Serifa LT
Printed and bound in China
by C&C Offset Printing Company
Limited

9 8 7 6 5 4 3 2 1

Photographic acknowledgements

Photographs © Zoë Lake 2022
except: p1 and 3 background ©
Khaneeros/Shutterstock 2021; p42
bl © Bangprikphoto/Shutterstock
2020; p60 © Elena Chevalier/
Shutterstock 2018; p70 bl © Ann in
the uk/Shutterstock 2018; 76 br ©
Purino/Shutterstock 2015; p78 ©
GOLFX/Shutterstock 2017; p102 br ©
Halfpoint/Shutterstock 2021; p104 ©
Victoriia Palii/Shutterstock 2019; p114
tr © ezhenaphoto/Shutterstock 2020;
p114 bl © Pressmaster/Shutterstock
2021; p124 © Dmytro Zinkevych/
Shutterstock 2019; p152 tr
© wavebreakmedia/Shutterstock
2019; Throughout paint brushstroke
© Sayan Puangkham/ Shutterstock
2021

Contents

Welcome

Have you ever noticed that on those unexpected, unplanned and gloriously lazy days, time seems to stretch out far more than on regular days, so often full of routine and fast-paced frenzy?

Well, my fun-loving family and I actually plan those unexpected days into our lives. We have to, otherwise they would never happen! And childhood is so incredibly precious – blink and it's gone. Quality family time is vital for nourishing the soul and for healthy growth, not just for youngsters but for us too.

By planning in that time for each other, those wonderfully sun-drenched summer days feel endless. In turn, these will create memories for the whole family, filled with fun and, most importantly, love.

A great passion of mine is creating something out of nothing, planning mini adventures with my ever-enthusiastic husband and persistently dancing daughter. I wrote this book to hopefully inspire you to create and plan your own mini adventures, which can be thrown together using what you already have, with very little notice.

Adventures at Home is packed with ideas to have fun with or without sunshine, without needing to spend much money or to travel far. It includes exciting ideas for activities and family-friendly recipes, whilst also considering the environment, encouraging the reusing and repurposing of items rather than buying new.

Time and imagination are the only two ingredients you really need to create memorable moments, a lesson worth passing along to the next generation. Oh, and a camera will also come in most useful.

However, most importantly, after becoming a parent time absolutely rockets by, so simply enjoy it all, wherever your family time takes you. Before you know it, you will be looking through your well-stocked photo albums, all warm and fuzzy from a life well lived.

Zoë Lake

Garden Music Festival

Unable to attend a live music festival to see friends play, we were inspired to make do at home and listened to the line-up on the radio instead. This had the added bonus that it was dog friendly, so Dex was happy too. You can easily achieve something similar with very little planning.

INGREDIENTS FOR A MEMORABLE DAY
- Tent • Duvets • Blankets • Cushions • Radio • Extension lead • Low tables
- Bunting • Lanyards • Wrist bands • Face paints • Festival food • Games & toys
- Safe lanterns • Fire pit • Sparklers

*Remember you don't have to have everything! Be creative and make do with what you have.

SETTING UP

We pitched the tent (very handy given the capricious British summertime), laid down the duvets and blankets, threw down the cushions and pillows, dragged the dog bed out and plugged in an extension cable for the radio. Many would stop there but that would be a shame . . .

We decided to go a step further and made lanyard VIP passes, allowing us unlimited access to the snack cupboard, a constant stream of tea and coffee, and also the use of a rather respectable lavatory without the need to queue. We also made matching festival wristbands from ribbon (see the DIY below) should we get lost in the garden.

Bunting was strung up amongst the foliage (DIY on page 45). We painted our faces with biodegradable glitter motifs and wore flowers in our hair. We drew temporary tattoos with face paints and a mehndi pen (you can use a washable ink pen instead).

We danced and boogied and snoozed. Half the toys in the house made their way out, making it difficult to find space to sit down by the end of the day, but totally worth it. There was even a festival wedding – Spiderman gave his daughter away to Steve; Barbie made a beautiful bride. It was all very moving.

HOW TO MAKE WRISTBANDS AND LANYARDS

To make your own lanyards, simply draw your design on to card cut to size, approximately 5cm (2in) by 10cm (4in). Get the youngsters to add the flourishing touches – our daughter drew flowers around ours.

We had spare laminating sheets, so chose to make them waterproof. Card works perfectly fine though, just use crayons or pencils for colouring the patterns and they won't run if the clouds decide to unleash. Punch a hole in the top and thread through a length of ribbon to

> Always save odds and ends of ribbon and string. Odd lengths used for flowers, clothes, gifts and tags come in very handy for projects like this.

fit around the neck; we added a matching bead here, just for fun.

Make festival wristbands out of the same patterned ribbon by simply tying a length around each person's wrist; we added a matching bead here too.

FOOD IDEAS

Why not set up a festival food station serving pizza or tacos, for example, where you can choose your own toppings and fillings. I won't judge, should you choose to set up a Pimm's tent. Get in some tropical juices you would not normally have at home like guava juice for the youngsters. These can always be watered down to reduce the sugar content or see page 133 for a raspberry fizz recipe.

LATER ON

When we had to retreat into our tent during a sudden rainstorm, our daughter complained that it didn't feel much like a festival anymore. We assured her that this was as authentic as it got. It was a good excuse to lounge around watching past live gigs online, a taster session for a real festival.

As the evening closed in, we piled on the layers and lit the firepit, turned the radio on low and listened together, discovering new bands and making a note of the tunes so that we could make a playlist later, as a reminder of our memorable day in the garden. You could light the lanterns and maybe crack open a pack of sparklers once the light wanes.

We like to spend as much time outside as we possibly can, winter is far too long for my liking. If your memory is as shoddy as mine, take plenty of photos of your day. These keepsakes will not only help you to remember what is important in life, but will serve as an excellent visual for your ever-growing children to keep their memories alive too.

OVERCAST?

Rain need not dampen your plans. Simply take it indoors. Make your lounge the acoustic tent. Drape scarves, keep the lighting low, put some recorded performances from Glasto on the big screen for a more authentic feel. Play those old LPs. Plus, there will be no need for wellies.

Record a Childhood Interview

Have you ever wanted to freeze-frame time? Those funny things our children say are priceless and often quickly forgotten. When our daughter was younger I took great joy jotting down those remarkable phrases, but soon she stopped talking nonsense. Now she tells us off for doing so.

Therefore, I decided to try and create some childhood gold with a recorded interview. And I was not disappointed. It's a wonderful keepsake, reminding us all how fun it is to dream big and have no reason to believe it won't work out. The magic is beyond price.

INGREDIENTS FOR A MEMORABLE DAY
- Recording device such as a camera or phone • Cosy area to set as a stage
- Notepad and pen • Interview questions

QUESTIONS

Write a set of questions (see overleaf for a few ideas), and have them nearby. There are different options for how to do this. You can either take the role of the interviewer, either in or out of shot. Or you can all huddle into the frame as a family and each take a set of questions, so that you play the interviewer and interviewee as well.

Your questions can be as simple or as wild as you like. In fact it's best if you go off on tangents in response to their answers as this opens up the conversation, adds more detail and often reveals the reasons behind their views.

SETTING UP

Set up a comfy spot for the interview. The sofa is an ideal place to fit everyone on; however, a bedroom is better as we probably all have a little difficulty in recalling what our childhood rooms looked like way back when. It's a treat looking back at books, posters, toys and games in the background, which inevitably will become long forgotten in adulthood. Oh, the heartbreak: at the time, you never think you will stop loving Bon Jovi.

If setting up elsewhere, pop a few favourite toys or cuddlies in shot of the camera as seeing much-loved toys again is just as important as the answers to the questions.

RECORD, STORE, COPY

Ok, ok, I still have a video camera, but hey, I don't need to worry about balancing my phone, so don't judge. Whatever way you choose to make memories, be sure to back them up, just in case. Even better, send the file to family and ask them to save it for a rainy day – only people that you completely trust. Nobody wants to see a video of their younger selves running around without any pants on at their wedding.

TOP TIPS

We still had our daughter's old, dismantled cot in the garage. We rebuilt it and left a side off, so that it was transformed into a bench. We threw some cushions on and as our youngster adores any kind of creature, her collection of furry friends was a must. Plus, it helped her to feel more comfortable with chatting candidly.

We set up outside in the summer holidays and had such a laugh recording information so vital, so pertinent, so important to such a young mind.

QUESTIONS FOR A CHILDHOOD INTERVIEW

- Name and age?
- What is your favourite colour?
- What thing are you really good at?
- What is your favourite toy?
- What do you want to do when you grow up?
- What pets do you have?
- What is your favourite book?
- What is your favourite TV series?
- What is your favourite film?
- What is your favourite animal?
- What do you want to learn?
- Do you know any other languages?
- Can you sing your favourite song?
- What is your favourite outfit?
- Which toys do you play with most?
- What is your favourite memory?
- What is your favourite drink?
- What is your favourite food?
- What do you love most about yourself?
- What is your favourite family activity?
- What makes you really happy?
- What advice would you give your future self?

> You could ask your child to hold up any recent drawings or art projects for the camera, as a way to document these glorious snippets of creativity.

WHATEVER THE WEATHER

Perhaps consider a favourite spot to conduct the interview. If your child loves the treehouse, set up the interview there. If another child prefers to do it at the beach, technology allows us to be flexible, so embrace it and go with the flow.

And maybe, just maybe, turn the tables and allow them to be the interviewer and ask you the tough questions!

Time Capsule

Another way to save memories is to create a time capsule; think of it as a snapshot of your family life at a particular time. Then set a date in the future when you can open it all together. It can include whatever you feel is most relevant, and of course, you could always make one each.

INGREDIENTS FOR A MEMORABLE DAY
- Two large plastic drinks bottles • Spray paint • Tape • Card for a label
- Photos and printed questionnaires • Small keepsakes and trinkets

---

MAKING THE CAPSULE

We raided our neighbour's recycling (we asked first of course). Two old plastic drinks bottles are fab for this job. I carefully cut them in half with a kitchen knife and sanded the sharp edges. Next, I spray painted them silver.

Plastic bottles offer ample room for knick-knacks and rolled up paper and photos. When the time comes, you simply fill one bottle, slightly squeeze the edge and push the other bottle over the top and tape together. We also added a label. We had spare laminating pouches, so laminated the label to ensure it stays put for a few years.

WHAT TO INCLUDE

You can include absolutely anything you like; you may even wish to upgrade to a box if you are a large family, but encourage everyone to throw something in, as while they may not be that interested now, they might feel left out in twenty years' time. Consider:

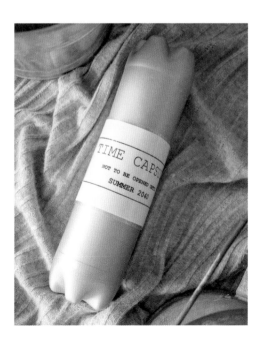

- Photos
- Completed questionnaires
- Small toys (not favourites)
- Tiny keepsakes
- Play jewellery
- Hand and footprints
- Artwork
- Photos of pets
- Family portrait
- Plans for the future
- Favourite meals and recipes
- Inspirational quotes

- Pressed flowers from your garden
- Natural treasures (like pebbles, nothing that can rot or go mouldy)
- Labels from favourite foods
- Newspaper clippings
- Birthday and anniversary cards

SAVING TREASURES

Be sure not to put anything inside that you will miss, as once it is sealed you must all agree to keep it that way until the date of the grand opening. Take your time collecting bits and pieces over a few weeks. For very young children, see if they can find enough small treasures to fill a matchbox, as small eyes often find tiny things that pass us by. It can be magical to come across these little snippets in time: the thrill of finding a fly's wing, only to unearth it again as an adult, can be wonderfully fulfilling.

STORAGE

I chose to recycle plastic for the casing. The best place to store it for us was our attic, but I'm quite heavy-handed whilst sifting through there periodically, so I did not want our capsule to be in a cardboard box that might get crushed.

Wherever you keep your time capsule, keep it dry, keep it safe. And maybe set a note for twenty years' time to have a family gathering and open up your history from an old plastic bottle.

CLEAR AND CLOUDLESS SKY?

If it is lovely weather, spend a bit of time taking photos or drawing your home and garden as both change quite often. When we moved in there was nothing but lawn and now we have mini forests staking their claim. It's often a pleasure to see how it all started out before the hard work.

Also, if you have an oak tree in your garden, take some leaf rubbings and pop in a few acorns. If you have roses, dry some petals to include. If you have a collection of shells and sea glass, throw a few in to remind you of your hobby.

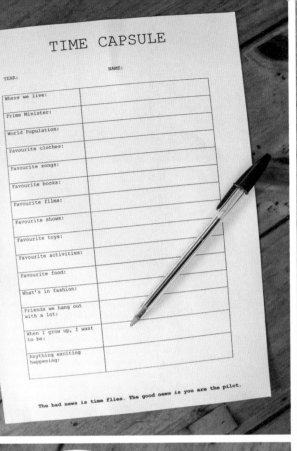

TIME CAPSULE

YEAR: NAME:

Where we live:	
Prime Minister:	
World Population:	
Favourite clothes:	
Favourite songs:	
Favourite books:	
Favourite films:	
Favourite shows:	
Favourite toys:	
Favourite activities:	
Favourite food:	
What's in fashion:	
Friends we hang out with a lot:	
When I grow up, I want to be:	
Anything exciting happening:	

The bad news is time flies. The good news is you are the pilot.

TIME CAPSULE
NOT TO BE OPENED UNTIL
SUMMER 2040

24 Hours without Electricity

This is a great activity for educating younger ones about the impact of energy and how to save it. It's a wonderful challenge to encourage youngsters to discover alternatives to activities that might otherwise use electricity.

INGREDIENTS FOR A MEMORABLE DAY
• Duvets • Blankets • Cushions • Books • Games • Low tables • Wooden board to create a sturdy surface • Baskets for carrying items • Crafts • Paints • Candles • Pack of cards • Snacks and an early midnight feast

---

Set yourself the goal to last twenty-four hours without any power at all; trust me, it is good fun. You will all be shouting 'noooo!' at each other whenever somebody grabs a phone to check something on Google or turns on a light switch out of habit.

This is a good opportunity to also discuss and discover new ways to make your home a little greener with simple eco swaps. Maybe make a list of small, easy changes such as using washable cloths instead of kitchen roll or purchasing wooden, compostable toothbrushes when your plastic ones need replacing (keep them for cleaning the home though!). It all helps. Encourage your children to come up with creative ideas.

SETTING UP

Perhaps start your day without any alarm clocks, eat only when you are hungry rather than because it is time to, and go to bed when you are tired. Take off your watches and unplug your clock if you wish, so that nobody knows what time it is!

If you can be outside, set up a quilt and make it comfy. The one pictured is an old stripy cover quilted on to a spare duvet, perfect for garden lounging. Archie approved immediately and settled himself for the day. We used our huge chopping board from a car boot sale as a table. It's great for colouring and playing games on – and for keeping your drinks safe-ish.

FOOD

Cook outside if you can. Planning your meals in advance will help; you could BBQ if the weather is kind. Having an outdoor fire and cooking over an open flame is fun (see page 26 for outdoor cooking ideas and page 30 for how to light a fire easily). We think that rifling through the camping gear for the gas stove is allowed if you have no other way of cooking outside.

If the thought of giving up gaming or phones for the day makes your children break out in hives, get them to write a meal plan and choose games to play. Involve them completely and give them jobs to do.

Get them on hot chocolate making duty (see opposite) or making jam jar lanterns for later on – glue tissue paper to the outside of clean deep jars and drop a tea light in for night-time ambience.

ACTIVITIES

Spend the day reading, writing, drawing, playing. You could create tin can phones, learn the alphabet in sign language, paint self-portraits, play hide-and-seek, croquet or badminton, make a bow and arrow from twigs, look through old photos, learn a magic trick, make jewellery, start an epic jigsaw to name just a few possible activities.

Dig out those forgotten board games, get creative with watercolour paints (see page 42 for inspiration), identify the flowers in your garden (see pages 56–7 for a few to get you started), match the leaves to the correct tree (pages 142–3), create a crazy family dance, secret handshake or elaborate fist bump.

Have a look through your books at home. Do you have any history books? Learn a few key dates in history. Found an atlas? Discover the location of countries you know the names of but are not quite sure where they are. Dusted off a dictionary? Learn a few new words and have fun attempting to weave them into conversation throughout the day. Use what you have at hand.

This is a good excuse to swat up on your knowledge of the night sky, so that when the light starts to wane, get star gazing. Once the first star appears, it's game on for spotting the next and the next. Binoculars will allow you to see the craters on the moon (see page 37 for star-gazing tips).

LATER ON

As the evening draws in, you could light the candles, douse yourself in natural insect repellent (recipe on page 121) and should clouds ruin your star-gazing fun, get out the playing cards and keep an eye on cheating sleeves. Snap and Sevens are good games for younger members of the family. If the weather turns, make a nest in the living room with cushions and tuck into the (albeit early) midnight feast by candlelight.

If the house is a bit chilly without the heating on, then stick the tent up indoors and sleep in there for the night; I can guarantee you will not be cold. You might not get any sleep either, what with elbows and knees in your chest; but that's just the way it goes.

OVERCAST?
The weather doesn't matter, simply move it indoors. Or stay on the move. Remember there is never the wrong weather, simply the wrong clothes. Tog up and set out for a nice long walk from home. This might wear you out enough that you will sleep through the night, regardless of that elbow in your chest.

HOT CHOCOLATE

We love this recipe in summer time around a campfire with the stars shining and also in winter, lying under the Christmas tree. Hot chocolate is one of those things in life that encapsulates childhood memories.

SERVES 4

Ingredients

- 1 litre (4 cups) hazelnut milk
- 1 heaped tbsp of cocoa or cacao powder
- 1 tbsp sugar or honey (or sweetener equivalent)

Directions

1. Pour the hazelnut milk into a pan and mix in the cocoa powder and sweetener of your choice.

2. Heat over the stove or an open fire.

3. The cocoa will float for a while, but as it heats up, it will start to dissolve and smell delicious. Be careful not to overheat and burn.

4. Serve warm in lovely generous mugs. Marshmallows optional.

Tiny Dolls' House

We found this old house in a charity shop for a couple of pounds. It clearly needed a little bit of love and I felt I was the person for the job. All it took was a lick of paint and a little bit of craft paper and job done! I used what I had at home and ended up not spending anything at all really.

However, there are so many wonderful tutorials online, you could quite easily build your own. It need not be anything fancy: a simple cube cut into compartments will create four rooms. Keep it flat at the top for a roof garden.

INGREDIENTS FOR A MEMORABLE DAY

• Dolls' house or build your own • Spare dolls' house furniture • Small items to repurpose as furniture and accessories • Scrap paint, carpet, wood, fabric and paper • Glue gun • Duct tape

---

MAKING A HOME

No matter whom your house is for, make it cosy. If you want to move in, you can guarantee that the miniature family will love it. And a dolls' house is something special that hopefully will be passed down through the generations, each time having a facelift, just as we do with our own homes.

WHAT TO USE

You can reuse and repurpose all manner of things, here are a few ideas:

- Any old dolls' house furniture you have at hand
- Magazine cut-outs for pictures, clocks and windows
- Corks as plant pots
- Clippings of faux foliage for plants
- Beads as vases
- Tiny dried flowers
- Fabric cut-offs for rugs, curtains and duvets
- Corks and stones as side tables
- Crystals and stones as ornaments
- String stuck to cardboard for mats and rugs
- Driftwood and lolly sticks for window ledges
- Curtain ring for wreath
- Empty glitter bottles as jugs or vases
- Twigs for towel rails or blanket holders
- String and miniature pegs for a washing line

If you get gift idea requests, perhaps suggest something for the dolls' house: tiny cupcakes on a tray, little books in a basket or even a teeny crocheted blanket will fuel the imagination.

- Lolly sticks for box planters with ground coffee glued in as mud
- Small vessels, baskets and boxes as decoration
- Earring hooks as lantern holders and curtain tie-backs

FURNITURE

If you don't have everything to hand, there's plenty you can make. We made a simple sofa from a cardboard box and added folded cardboard as arms, rounded with wadding. The upholstery is an old shirt simply duct-taped underneath. I added cut-down cork casters. The cushions were made from an old jumper, cut down and stuffed with a teeny bit of wadding.

The bed is a simple upturned cardboard apple box. The headboard was made from scrap wood found in our firepit. You can make a simple table from lolly sticks cut to size, corks for feet or long matchsticks as legs. Lolly sticks also make great benches with matchsticks as legs. And, if you're ambitious, fabulous parquet flooring too!

SMALLER ITEMS

You could make flowers from tissue paper or clay. Dried flowers are brilliant too. You can make small bread loaves and baguettes from salt dough. Blankets are super quick to knit by hand and make precious keepsakes. Cover a cork in twine to make a natural plant pot.

Fray the edges of scraps of fabric for rugs. Cut up old clothes for throws, bed toppers and towels. We even made a broom from a twig and some old dried grass found in our garden. Engage the imagination and repurpose any kind of small item, turning a discarded dolls' house into a cherished toy.

CLEAR AND CLOUDLESS SKY?

This dolls' house rotates around the house and garden. As time goes on, we collect additional items for it and these are now housed in a palm leaf basket that travels around with it. That way, we can set up shop anywhere relatively easily.

Throw down a blanket, maybe use a folding tray or low table, and you can set up play anywhere. It might not stop there though. The whole family could get involved in making additional items – like a treehouse, BBQ area, tent. You can only be held back by your imagination.

Cook Outdoors

We love cooking outdoors in the fresh air. When cooking outside there are several options to make any mealtime memorable. Perhaps make breakfast outside early in the morning on the gas stove. The tuneful whistling kettle magically transports you to a camping field in the middle of nowhere, accompanied by cheerful birdsong.

Or BBQ at lunchtime in the sunshine, making your neighbours green with envy as the scent of deliciousness wafts over the fence.

Or you could make paella or curry in the open air in the evening. Potatoes wrapped in foil and stuffed under the embers of an evening bonfire is a timeless trick. Simply leave them for half an hour and dress with grated cheese, allowing it to melt into all the crevices. Accompany with dough sticks – bread cooked on a stick over the fire (page 97); they're great fun to make.

SETTING UP

There is nothing quite as special as cooking over an open fire. It does not require too much effort either. Our firepit was super simple to make, using large rocks from a discarded rockery. We arranged them in a circle and laid down some sand in the middle and voilá. We have had a few firepits over the years; however, this is by far the best one yet. Please be careful when using a rock surround. Ensure they are not soft rocks to avoid them exploding in the heat! Or create a dedicated outdoor kitchen (shown overleaf) for making the most of every mealtime opportunity.

EQUIPMENT NEEDED

You will need a sturdy grill rack to cook upon. An old oven rack or cake cooling rack laid on the stones will do the trick, if you cannot find one with a stand.

We only use cast iron pots and pans outside as they are heavier and sturdier, and therefore more difficult to knock over should a young one race past or want to stir a little overzealously. Any old pan will do though; just remember they are more likely to be blackened on an open fire.

Investing in a pair of fireproof gloves is a wise move – for lifting pots and pans safely and refuelling the fire. Ours are bright red and do the job of shouting out the message of 'safety first'.

An old enamel teapot is perfect for hot chocolate (see page 21) and don't forget the toasted marshmallows – a highlight for young'uns and oldies alike.

FOOD

Start your fire and allow it to establish before you start cooking. Avoid fuel-soaked fire
starters as they can give off harmful fumes which are not great for cooking on (see
overleaf for tips on starting a fire). Our firepit is located next to our chicken run, so whilst
waiting for the fire to get going, the inquisitive ladies often join us for a quick snooze
on our laps – the ultimate way to unwind. Keeping chickens is most beneficial for your
mental health – they are both hilarious and fascinating creatures!

One-pot cooking is the easiest option (see page 31 for a tasty firepit stew – no chickens
required). However, making a quick couscous with lemon and coriander takes no time;
add that to a plate of flat mushrooms, veggie sausages or organic meat plus a side salad
which can be prepared outside and you've made a feast. Most recipes can be adapted to
cooking over a naked flame.

To make the most of your adventures, remember to involve the youngsters in your
plans. Don't cook all the food yourself on the open fire, teach them about safety and allow
them to collect twigs and logs before you begin, get them to stir the cooking pot carefully
and refuel the skewers with marshmallows. Children will enjoy the experience much more
if they are actively involved. This also goes for tidying up afterwards too! Life lessons are
all around us.

OVERCAST?
Do you really need your tools in the shed? Can you move them to
the garage? Well, ok then. Now convert that lacklustre shed into a
beautiful dining area. Painting it white inside and adding a mirror will
bounce the light around. Add folding chairs and a table, and fairy lights
too. Perfect. Even if you cannot cook outside, maybe you can create an
area under cover to enjoy your meal instead.

Lighting a Fire

Always maintain a 'safety first, then fun' approach. Youngsters should be taught to respect fire from a young age and the dangers that can come with it. Once this is second nature, they can start to be given responsibility when lighting the fire – until then they can certainly help build it.

INGREDIENTS FOR MAKING A FIRE
• Torn recycled cardboard and paper • Kindling wood, dry twigs, leaves and pinecones • Seasoned or kiln-dried logs • Long matches or lighter

---

1. The first stage is simple – collect and store your supplies. Whenever anything is delivered in plain cardboard boxes, envelopes or tissue paper, we shred it into small bits and dry store it in our Halloween cauldron, ensuring the cauldron is used year-round.

    For kindling, save a pile of sticks from the garden and store under cover. Dried leaves are perfect for starting a flame and pinecones smell lovely and are easy to burn; we collect ours from the local park each season before their industrial lawn mower chomps them all up. Youngsters can easily help out with this part.

    We also save our pistachio shells and ice cream sticks. Alternatively purchase a sack of kindling from your local garden centre. Be sure to keep your kindling and dried logs under cover. Damp logs will only cause tension with your neighbours as you smoke the street out.

2. When ready to start your fire, make a small mound of cardboard in the middle of your pit, stack dry twigs or kindling around it. Youngsters can help with this stage too.

3. Light the cardboard with a long match or long lighter. Remember, fire needs air holes for oxygen to help it breathe. If using extra-long matches or lighting sticks, you might allow older children to help with this stage, as long as you think they are responsible enough. As the flames start to lick the kindling, add a few more pieces of kindling to feed the fire.

4. As the fire starts to grow, add a small dry log on top, taking care not to flatten your burning mound. Larger logs can be added later, once the fire becomes more established. Carefully blow the base of the fire to get more oxygen in. If you're lucky like me, your in-laws might give you a marvellous pair of good old-fashioned bellows for your birthday; this makes light work of getting a fire going.

FIREPIT STEW

This recipe has been created so that you can just chuck it all together in one pan for ease.

Afterwards, tell stories around the fire with full bellies. Alternatively, take it in turns to make up the next line in a story, and then pass it on to the next person – who knows where you might end up?

SERVES 4–6

Ingredients

- Can of cannellini beans or butter beans
- Can of chickpeas
- Can of black-eyed beans or borlotti beans
- Two cans of tinned tomatoes
- Jar of sundried tomato paste approx. 190g (4 tbsp)
- One glass of red wine
- Glug of garlic-infused olive oil
- Pinch of smoked salt
- 2 tsp smoked paprika
- ½ tsp cumin

Directions

1. Start your fire and when established but not setting any nearby hedging alight, add the grill rack. Make sure it is sturdy!

2. Empty the ingredients into a big, deep pan and give it a good stir. Carefully move the pan to the heat.

3. Keep stirring every 1–3 minutes with a wooden spoon, keeping the lid on between stirs. Uncover after 10 minutes and continue to cook for a further 10–20 minutes (still stirring frequently), until it is thoroughly cooked through and starting to thicken.

4. Remove from the heat. Leave to stand for 20 minutes before serving; this will give it the chance to really thicken up.

5. Serve with sun-dried tomato dough sticks (see page 97).

Feel free to omit the red wine. Most of the alcohol will be burned off during cooking and it adds a lovely depth of flavour, but it is not essential.

Disco Fever

Indoor discos are a staple in our house. It all started when a kind relative DJ'd our wedding (it was awesome – AC/DC all the way!) and afterwards said, 'Hey, keep the disco lights.' Best sentence ever.

We regularly put them up for a spontaneous boogie, but you can guarantee to see them each birthday, Christmas and New Year as well as most winter weekends.

INGREDIENTS FOR A MEMORABLE DAY

• Disco lights • Mirror ball • Snow projector • Snacks • Drinks • Muscles to clear your furniture to the sides • Cushions to cover hard surfaces like fire hearths • Your dancing shoes • Insanely obsessed dog optional

---

CREATE A PLAYLIST

Spend time as a family creating the perfect playlist, giving everyone the chance to add their favourites. Anything goes. No arguments.

Once created, clear the furniture and close the curtains. Make sure you have snacks and drinks available, maybe even some home-made crisps (recipe on page 35) and a jug of water on standby. And jelly of course. Jelly is suitable for any occasion.

TURN DOWN THE LIGHTS

You may find you own one or two disco lights already, but if you do invest in lights, think hard about how you might use them. For example, our white snow projector light can also be used for Christmas decoration as well. Make your investment work for you.

We also move in our daughter's lights from her room, such as the small disco ball in the corner here and a mirror ball. I would be lying if I said the moon light was hers. It's really not. It's mine and she's not having it. We also have an inexpensive disco bulb which fits into the top light. That's the dog's. He loves it.

CHOREOGRAPH A DANCE

If you are feeling brave, create your own family dance and spontaneously jump into action at the next family party. We've not done this, but be sure to send me your videos should you choose to go down this route.

MAKE IT REGULAR

In the winter, exercise can sometimes be a drag but not if you own disco lights. A thirty-minute session will have you feeling pain in muscles you didn't know existed, but it's totally worth it. This will definitely count towards your aerobic exercise.

If a young one is having a tough day, leave them a note asking them to meet you in the kitchen (or any unexpected place). Switch off all the lights, and when they enter, turn your disco lights on and press play with the music. An unexpected boogie can work wonders for woes.

CLEAR AND CLOUDLESS SKY?

If you have a garage or a gazebo, set it up and get boogying. Or if you're lucky enough to live somewhere there is no risk of upsetting the neighbours with the noise, take a speaker outside and project your lights on to the trees, it looks lovely.

In fact, if you can't beat them, join them. One evening, when our neighbours were having a wedding reception in their back garden, after the elders went home, they cranked up the volume and upped the tempo. Did we mind? Not one bit. We dug our disco lights out, pointed them at our hedge and threw down some moves ourselves.

HOME-MADE CRISPS

Try sliced parsnips, carrots, beetroot and sweet potato for a truly colourful snack. They will crisp up at different speeds so keep checking them and remove them when ready – before they burn.

Using the mandoline blade on my trusty processor, I find that three medium potatoes fit perfectly on to one large baking tray and keeps the three of us happy for a snack. You can always add more; just adjust your cooking time to allow a little longer for the crisps on the bottom shelf to crisp up.

MAKES ENOUGH FOR 3–4 PEOPLE

Ingredients

- 3–4 medium sized potatoes
- 1 tbsp olive oil
- Generous pinch of salt

Directions

1. Preheat the oven to 200°C / Fan 180°C / Gas 6 / 400°F.
2. Using a mandoline slicer or the mandoline blade on a food processor, slice the potatoes finely. Alternatively use a sharp knife to cut very thin rounds.
3. Dry the potatoes on a clean tea towel, removing any moisture.
4. In a large bowl, mix the salt and oil and then throw in the potato slices. Mix well with your hands, coating both sides.
5. Lay the slices out on a baking tray (or two); they can touch but not overlap.
6. Bake your crisps for 15–20 minutes, removing those that start to brown as, depending on the thickness, some may need longer. I also find every oven different so feel free to check every couple of minutes – our daughter usually sits by the oven window waiting and watching, she's a brilliant timer.
7. Allow to cool for a minute and serve with a sprinkle of salt or cracked black pepper.

Alternatively, when mixing the potatoes in with the oil, you could add a generous grind of black pepper for a fiery snack or throw a tablespoon of vinegar in the bowl, a teaspoon of herbs, or try a flavoured oil such as truffle or even chilli oil for a real kick.

Star Gazing

Our daughter fondly remembers these highlights of the summer calendar – the winter too, although usually for getting so chilly that we race each other back indoors to the warmth! Star gazing is such a simple pleasure, encouraging youngsters to look up and wonder at the skies, as our ancestors have done for millennia.

INGREDIENTS FOR A MEMORABLE NIGHT
• Inflatable paddling pool or airbed • Duvets and blankets • Pillows • Woolly hats
• Hot water bottles • Star guides – books or apps • Torch • Snacks • Warm layers

---

SETTING UP

We like to enjoy star-gazing nights lying in an old inflatable paddling pool filled with spare duvets – it was punctured years ago, but patched with reliable duct tape, it still serves us well by keeping the chill out when it turns cold. However, a simple blanket will do.

The best way to enjoy the stars is on your back, so make sure your nest is warm and dry. Keep lots of layers nearby to keep your core warm. Add the next layer before you get too cold; that way, you keep the heat in.

Make hot water bottles for everyone. You may not need them at first, but if the chill starts to creep in later on, unwrapping a 'hottie bottie' from a spare blanket will be most welcome.

In my opinion, woolly hats are a must, regardless of time of year or weather.

We also like to accompany the evening with some sort of early midnight feast – rock cakes (see page 49) have served us well over the years.

Turn out all the lights, candles too, and let your eyes become accustomed but keep a torch nearby for toilet trips. Who will spot the first shooting star?

HELPFUL GUIDES

There are lots of apps to help you identify constellations and satellites. Sometimes the constellations take a bit of figuring out, such as Pegasus, the winged horse, that makes more sense when you know he is upside down. These apps help to show you an artist's impression of the creature or person that many of the constellations are named after. Books are fabulous for this too, just remember the torch so that you can read them!

CONSTELLATIONS

Constellations are stars that have been grouped together over the ages, to depict stories, beliefs, myths and legends.

There are a few easy constellations to spot to get your bearings (see pages 40–1 for some to start with). The Plough is the most obvious, like a frying pan shape; it is part of the Great Bear constellation (*Ursa Major*). However, ancient Britons saw it as a chariot racing across the sky.

From here, you can easily find the Little Bear (*Ursa Minor*) above it – a smaller, reversed reflection of the Plough. From here, you will find the seemingly stationary North Star or Polaris at the end of the pan handle or Little Bear's tail.

MYTH AND LEGEND

The constellations all have wonderful tales behind them. A few are worth researching beforehand so you can impress the family later.

For example, Cancer the Crab, which can be visible as an upside-down Y, represents the crab Karkinos. The goddess Hera is said to have sent Karkinos to distract the hero Hercules when he was fighting the Hydra, a monstrous serpent with many heads. It did not work. Apparently, Hercules kicked the crab so hard, it flew all the way into the sky!

DIFFERENT TALES TO TELL

Different cultures have different takes on the constellations, but each civilization over the ages has tried to make sense of the stars above us, associating them with their beliefs or traditional stories.

Some see Boötes as the herdsmen, herding the nearby Great Bear and Little Bear, but in another myth he is Arcas, the son of the god Zeus and his mistress Calisto.

Ancient Greeks believed that Arcas was turned into a constellation along with his mother, whom Zeus had turned into a bear, to hide her from his wife Hera. When Arcas started unwittingly hunting his mother in the woods one day, Zeus avoided the bloodshed by turning them both into constellations.

THE MOON

You can always check the phases of the moon beforehand. A full moon means a glorious view of the lunar craters and dry seas (binoculars will help out here); however, it does not make for a good star-gazing evening as it will be too bright.

If it is a full moon, it is a wonderful excuse to pencil in another star-gazing session in two weeks' time, when it will be a new moon and a guaranteed darker sky.

PLANETS

The brightest star in the sky is not actually a star but our neighbouring planet Venus, named after the goddess of love. You can often see Mars and Jupiter too. Mars appears distinctly red in our night sky.

Did you know that all of the planets in our solar system would actually fit inside Jupiter with room to spare? Jupiter's volume is the equivalent of 1,300 Earths. It makes my brain hurt.

GALAXIES

If it is a really dark night, you can often make out a hazy band stretching across our sky. This is our galaxy, the Milky Way. You are seeing it from inside one of the arms of the spiral. If you are very lucky, you may see a small smudge below Cassiopeia; this is a collection of billions of stars, making up our nearest spiral galaxy, called Andromeda, named after a princess.

SHOOTING STARS

Most nights you will see a rogue shooting star, or meteor – don't forget to make a wish. Look out for meteor showers at certain times of year when you should be able to see several in one night. The Perseids are seen each year between mid-July and mid-August; check online for the best dates to view them at their brightest.

ISS AND SATELLITES

Also look online for when the International Space Station might be visible overhead. And watch out for satellites going over too; they are like shooting stars but move slowly across the sky. This – and bat-spotting – is probably our daughter's favourite night sky activity.

SLEEP UNDER THE STARS

If the youngsters fall asleep, no worries. Sleeping under the stars is a wonderful treat, just make sure they are warm and cosy. You may all want to make a night of it and sleep under our star laden sky. Sleeping bags are great for this, and woolly hats are a definite must!

Or even better, if like us you have been star gazing in an old inflatable paddling pool, then this makes for a perfect outdoor bed, keeping the breeze out. Fill with several duvets as mattresses, then soft pillows and a big duvet on top. There's even room for a quietly snoozing dog.

We did, however, find that our bed had deflated further one morning. At around 4 a.m., with the birds singing, our kitten Poe thought she would join us and jumped up, on to the side. Out came the duct tape again.

OVERCAST?

Clouds are no good for star gazing. However, if it is just too cold to be outside, pick a window with a darkened view of the sky – no street lamps – and discover what you can see.

Don't let winter put you off. You may not be able to spend the night sleeping under the stars, but the crisp, cold skies will mean a great sight of Orion's belt, made up of three stars, containing the red supergiant Betelgeuse – a star with a diameter 700 times bigger than our sun! If it goes supernova, it will glow as bright as our moon for months.

DRACO – The Dragon

One of the largest constellations, it wraps around Polaris, across half of the sky. The head is more identifiable than the snaking body, as the four stars of the head are much brighter. Children will love to spot the dragon flying overhead.

CASSIOPEIA – The Queen

From Greek mythology, Cassiopeia was going to turn over her own daughter, Andromeda, to a sea monster, so she was not one to be trusted. However, her name lives on in the easily identifiable set of five stars making a large W in the sky. Nearby, if you look below the W, you may be able to see the Andromeda galaxy, our nearest galaxy – a mere 2.5 million light years away.

BOÖTES – The Hunter

The hunter is large and easy to spot in the sky; his diamond-shaped body is the easiest part to see, with the bright star Arcturus at the base. His trusty dogs are also nearby – *Canis Venatici*. He is also known as the herdsman and is said to be herding the bears in the sky – *Ursa Major* and *Ursa Minor*.

CYGNUS – The Swan

Another easy constellation to find, sometimes called the Northern Cross. The swan is said to have been one of the disguises that the Greek god Zeus used for sneaking off, undetectable to his wife Hera. However, this large-winged bird is a fun and easy shape for youngsters to spot.

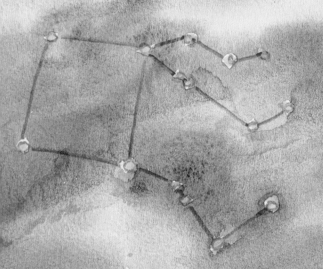

THE PLOUGH – Part of the Great Bear

The seven stars that make up the Plough are very bright and easy to find. They make a saucepan shape with a bent handle that is always clearly visible in the night sky. It makes up the main body of the Great Bear in the *Ursa Major* constellation. You can follow the direction of the Plough's handle to find the bright star Arcturus.

CORONA BOREALIS – The Crown

Located near to Boötes, this distinctive celestial crown is fun to find. Princess Ariadne is said to have thrown her crown into the sky in celebration of her wedding to the Greek god Bacchus.

PEGASUS – The Winged Horse

The stars making up the Great Square of Pegasus are easily visible in the sky. However, the front of the horse only makes sense once you realize you are looking at it upside down! The Pegasus is said to have been born when Perseus chopped off Medusa's head.

URSA MINOR – The Little Bear

The tail of the Little Bear curves in the opposite direction to the Great Bear. The last star in the tail is Polaris, often known as the North Star. It is not particularly bright; however, Polaris stays still, as it lies on the axis of the Earth's spin, which means all the other objects in the sky rotate around it, making it very handy for navigating without SatNav.

Art Session

We spent a lovely afternoon painting this glorious orchid, which seemed to flower for most of the year. It may very well be flowering still as you read these pages.

INGREDIENTS FOR A MEMORABLE DAY
- Canvas boards or art paper • Medium of your choice – paints, pastels or pencils
- Paint brushes and water jar • Old tablecloth or sheet • Vase or jam jar
- Fresh flowers • Old shirts to wear back to front for youngsters or old clothes
- Canapé tray and canapés • Sherry glasses and fizz • Classical music
- Paper and pen for artist bios

SETTING UP

If you are lucky enough to have blooms in your garden – daffs, primroses, branches in blossom, interesting foliage, roses, hydrangea, even the humble dandelion, gather a few stems and pop them in a vase or jam jar (pages 56–7 show a few common flowers that you might find in your garden).

Next throw an old tablecloth over the table and place the vase in the middle, so that everyone can see the display. Then choose your medium – pencils, charcoal, pastels, poster paint, watercolours, oils, acrylics, whatever takes your fancy. Once you are all set, gather around the table and unleash your creativity.

GETTING CREATIVE

There is no right or wrong way when being creative. We all see things differently; therefore, encourage children to develop their own style and approach.

Glass jars and detailed blooms can be difficult for young ones to copy, so encourage creative licence and see how they might bend the rules.

It does not have to be flowers that you paint, but they do brighten dark corners. They also make excellent gifts for friends and family when celebrations roll round. Add some shading and shadows to make pictures really come to life.

MAKING IT REGULAR

You could make this a regular event at home; perhaps challenge yourselves to learn about a different artist each month and attempt to create each piece in their style – think Matisse, Van Gogh, Monet, Picasso and Seurat for fun techniques. Or invite grandparents or other family round to have a go next time, making it a real family affair.

HOLD AN EXHIBITION

Once you have finished, display your works of art in the living room. Invite friends and family over for an art exhibition.

Encourage the youngsters to display other pieces of art or sculpture that they have created alongside. Write an artist bio next to a mini self-portrait or photograph, listing their likes and dislikes for fun.

Get the youngsters to write a welcome sign, put up some bunting (DIY opposite), play classical music in the background and arrange simple canapés on a dish. Thin slices of cheese and tomato stacked on small savoury biscuits or slices of cucumber and cream cheese on toast rounds are all good choices.

Pass around a tray of raspberry fizz (recipe on page 133) served in sherry glasses and feel the decadence.

CLEAR AND CLOUDLESS SKY?

If the weather is beautiful, take the painting session outside. We have a dedicated blanket for painting outdoors. That way, there is no need to be precious about spilling a jar of painty water, which inevitably happens. You could even paint a scene from the garden.

Alternatively, just let the youngsters use their imagination. One of my favourite pieces of all time was painted in the garden. It is titled The Unicorn and the Frog – the brainchild of a very focused three-year-old, who feverishly worked away to complete her masterpiece, green paint swiped across her forehead. This is how treasured memories are made.

If you live near a park, a beach, woodland or open gardens, then next time you're out, remember to pack a simple bag with art supplies – either a notepad and a few pencils, or a watercolour paper pad, watercolour paints, brushes and a jar with water (ensure it has a tight lid), so that you can set up and paint outdoors.

Making Bunting

We have so much bunting in our house. Some up permanently, other lengths stored away for special occasions such as for parties and birthday celebrations. I even carry a small amount of bunting neatly folded and stored in my bag, just in case we should ever need it for an impromptu party vibe whilst out and about.

YOU WILL NEED
- Triangle template • Old fabric or swatches of material • Bunting tape or thick ribbon
- Needle and thread or sewing machine • Pins

Bunting sets a celebratory scene and there's no need to spend money buying a set of bunting as making your own costs next to nothing. I make mine from old fabric swatch books, donated by friends, but you could use old clothes, sheets, cushion covers or similar.

1. Use a card or paper template for your bunting triangle and cut around it whilst it is pinned to the fabric. I'm such a sucker for bunting that my husband – dedicated to the cause – made me my very own template out of a triangle of plywood, topped with a drawer handle for many years' worth of bunting making, but a cardboard template works just as well.

2. Lay out the cut triangles and arrange them into the desired order. Then, evenly spacing them apart, pin them to the bunting tape or ribbon. The tape can be folded over the triangles or the triangles sewn behind it, whichever you prefer. Ensure you leave enough tape at each end to tie a loop for hanging.

3. Next sew your triangles on to the tape using a simple straight stitch. A machine will make fast work of this; however, quietly hand-sewing in the evening, when the youngsters are in bed, can be wonderfully calming . . . until you stab your finger.

4. Hang the bunting and admire the cheeriness. Angus, the budgie, clearly approved (see opposite page).

Cream Tea Party

Who needs a reason to have a cream tea? What's not to love: tiny cakes and teeny sandwiches on pretty plates and sweet tea in ridiculously fragile teacups, with raised pinky if we're getting serious about it. You may not be able to leave for quite some time afterwards as cream teas do tend to revolve around carbohydrates. However, making the time to slow down and appreciate the age-old ritual of afternoon tea is completely worth a full belly.

INGREDIENTS FOR A MEMORABLE DAY
- Tablecloth • Teapot and tea cosy • Teacups, saucers and small plates
- Fancy glasses • Cake stand • Vase of flowers • Bunting and flags
- Jugs for drinks • Music • Cloth napkins

SETTING UP

If you do not have any outdoor seating, you could drag out chairs and tables and rugs from inside. Instead of single-use paper napkins, use washable cloth or linen napkins or even use pretty tea towels which are a perfect size for covering small children, and clumsy grown-ups too (see page 51 for DIY napkin roses).

DECORATIONS

Think dainty teacups, cake stands, pretty fabrics and crystal glasses, which all help to set the scene. Hang the bunting (DIY on page 45), or get the younger ones involved by decorating triangles of paper to fold at the top and glue on to string. If it's a royal occasion or perhaps a sporting event, get the flags out. Scour the garden for some pretty blooms to pop in a vase or a clean jar. A colourful tablecloth, or in this case a remnant of unhemmed floral fabric, is a prerequisite of teatime dining.

FOOD

There are plenty of classic finger foods that can be made by little hands (see page 50 for ideas). Jelly and ice cream served in teacups is fun. Sorbet in sherry glasses looks divine. Of course, do not forget the scones. Whether you choose to put clotted cream or jam first, there will be no judgement here. I am a big fan of both Cornish sand dunes and the Dorset Jurassic coast.

DRINKS AND MUSIC

A hot pot of tea is paramount, preferably with a tea cosy (ours looks like a chicken in case you were wondering). Equally so, a glass of fizz, a refreshing G&T or a jug of Pimm's for

the elders taking part are all possibilities. A vibrant pink traditional lemonade for the youngsters is wonderfully colourful or a fizzy cordial made from raspberries (see recipe on page 133). We like to play Vera Lynn quietly in the background or something light and classical with violins: very English garden. Simply add glorious sunshine to complete the look and feel.

ATTIRE

Why not dress up for the occasion? Gentlemen could wear shirts, bow tie optional. Ladies, go to town – floral frocks, forties-style hair and a bright red lipstick. Fascinators are encouraged where tiaras are not available.

CHARITY SHOPPING FOR SUPPLIES

As a way to keep costs low and stay as green as you can, recycle, reuse and repurpose where you are able. When you can't, supporting your local charity shops benefits everyone.

Not only can you purchase incredible supplies from charity shops, such as second-hand crockery and cut-glass crystal, patterned fabric for home-made bunting and hand-sketched books for identifying flora and fauna, to name a few. But you will also be supporting worthwhile causes whilst saving money.

When shopping second-hand, you never know what you might find. You may stumble upon a glass chandelier for a few pennies and, all of a sudden, you're having an evening of exquisite Arabian dining in a marquee made of sheets, the chandelier hanging splendidly as the centrepiece, a collection of rugs below your feet with twinkling tealights all around. The wonderful aromas of hummus, tabbouleh, haloumi, falafels and pomegranate tempting the senses. You just need a little inspiration, often found in a trusty charity shop.

OVERCAST?

A cream tea will taste marvellous wherever you eat it, so no need to worry if the weather does not play ball. Decorate the table indoors with blooms, dot a few sturdy tea light holders around and move your bunting inside. Pretend you are dining at the finest hotel in London, darling.

ROCK CAKES

These are super easy to make, and as there is no need to make them look good, they are great for little hands to dollop on to the baking tray.

If you are feeling naughty, replace the sultanas with chocolate chips.

Always try to source your eggs from a free range, organic supplier. Not only do they taste miles better, with brighter yolks, but happy chickens make the world a much better place.

MAKES 12

Ingredients

- 200g (1¾ cups) self-raising flour
- 50g (¼ cup) sugar (or replacement equivalent)
- 1 tsp baking powder
- 100g (1 stick) softened butter (or vegan version)
- 150g (1 cup) sultanas
- 1 egg (or for vegan, one mashed banana)
- 1 tsp vanilla extract
- 1 tbsp milk to combine (or non-moo milk)

Directions

1. Preheat oven to 180°C / Fan 160°C / Gas 4 / 350°F. Pop in the baking tray to warm up.

2. Combine the dry ingredients in a bowl. Then add the wet ingredients. Add the milk to help it stick together.

3. Take the baking tray out of the oven and grease with a little butter, which should just melt easily as you swipe the tray. It won't be long before the tray is cool enough to handle again.

4. Scoop a tablespoon of mixture on to the tray and space the mounds evenly apart as they will spread in the oven. There's no need to make them look pretty, or they won't look like rocks.

5. Bake for 15–20 minutes. Cool on a rack.

Cream Tea Menu

Crustless sandwiches with fillings (freeze the crusts for French toast another day):

- Egg and cress
- Brie and cranberry
- Classic cucumber
- Smoked salmon and cream cheese
- Tuna mayo
- Cherry tomato and cheese

Our daughter is obsessed with jam sandwiches – making your own jam is optional.

Decorate cupcakes with a chocolate flake or a classic cherry on top.

Star-shaped seeded cheese scones look great stacked on a tiered stand.

We love rock cakes for any occasion (see previous page).

Butterfly cakes will leave a lasting memory and are fun to make.

A Victoria sandwich topped with fresh strawberries is always a showstopper.

Simple sliced cheese on water biscuits are easy for small hands to assemble.

And don't forget clotted cream scones topped with yummy strawberry jam – or vice versa.

Basil, cherry tomato and mozzarella on toast rounds are very cute.

Cloth Napkin Rose

1. Take a square cloth napkin.

2. Fold over – not quite in half to leave a small overlap behind.

3. Roll up from the bottom, leaving a small triangle at the top.

4. Next roll from right to left.

5. Tuck the edge into the fold where you can.

6. Turn upside down and pull the rose leaf triangles out to support the rose on your plate.

Reading Nook

One of the best ways to help to expand your children's minds is to get them reading. Let them get lost in another time, in another realm. The gift of books is never to be underestimated. Stories stay with us and can encourage play.

INGREDIENTS FOR A MEMORABLE DAY
- Tepee, tent or den • Blankets and cushions • Basket of books • Snacks
- Leakproof water bottles • Cuddly toys • Imagination

What better way to spend a lazy afternoon than with a book in one hand and your children bundled on your lap, hanging on your every word, lost in another world. Make the most of it. Before too long, you will be buried under limbs, and inevitably, the day will come when instead of sitting on you, or lovingly beside you, they will be the other end of the sofa with their feet on you. It's ok, it happens to us all.

SETTING UP

Until that day comes, we like to make a den to read in, or a reading nook. This can be as simple as piling a mound of cushions on the bed and snuggling in or go all out to create a dedicated hidey hole with a basket of books nearby.

We tend to use the tepee when the weather is nice. I made this many years ago and it is still holding up well. You can use blankets and net curtains for mats to set the tone. A snoozing dog and inquiring tortoise are optional. Dex is never far away, and Logan, the tortoise, often pops up every now and then to find out what's happening.

ACTIVITIES

If your child is just starting to read, grab an armful of their furry friends off the bed and encourage them to read to their cuddly toys at 'school'. You could even make workbooks from folded paper to ensure that 'the students' are all paying attention.

Older children may like to write their own stories, whilst hidden away from prying eyes, not unlike Anne from the novel *Anne of Green Gables*.

We were fortunate enough to be sent a box full of old Ladybird books from a friend. The stories are timeless and the language used instantly transports you into another era: when spindles were to be feared, when you weren't quite certain that seed would grow into a plant or something else entirely, and feasts and balls were just part of your average day. Alas, your timepiece striking midnight might cause trouble.

Just be aware of scary stories before bed. Even something that may seem important, such as a book on climate change, may not be the best choice at bedtime. While such topics certainly have their place, children should not have to not worry about fixing the world as they drift off to sleep. The action plan can wait until morning.

FOOD AND DRINKS

Keep snacks simple and nearby such as carrot sticks in a jar or container which can be sealed shut again afterwards. Use bottles for drinks if you can, to avoid spills on the pages. Frozen 'sweeties' such as puréed strawberry and gelatine, frozen in ice cube trays, are a welcome summer treat. Or mix your favourite nut butter, steel cut oats and honey or rice malt syrup, refrigerate and then cut them into squares. Or for older ones, frozen grapes are a wonderful snack – simply cut them in half to make them safer to munch on.

MAKING A HIDEAWAY

The tepee (opposite) was made from old duvet covers from a charity shop and bamboo canes. The covers were cut to size and I sewed some pockets along the edges to hold upright canes. These were all tied at the top with elastic bands. I also added further pockets at the base for additional canes to give more stability. This project requires only basic sewing and can easily be assembled in one evening whilst the youngsters are tucked up for the night.

A simple alternative is rope strung across two trees with a sheet thrown over, then weighted down with rocks to create a simple ridge tent. It is easy to build and gives youngsters somewhere to call their own.

Pick a few flowers to make it feel homely (see pages 56–7 for common garden blooms and their meanings) and cosy up as you are transported to another world.

OVERCAST?

You could make a nook under the dining table (see page 64 for a DIY tablecloth den) or hang sheets over the clothes dryers indoors. Two dining chairs turned around and covered with a blanket become magical with some battery-operated string lights inside.

We keep a basket of old tablecloths, curtains and scarves, along with a pot of pegs, for creating little hideaways when the weather is a bit rubbish. Perfect for rainy days.

Garden Flowers

DAISY *Bellis perennis*
Daisies symbolize innocence, purity and love. Their simplicity and resilience reflect childhood innocence well, as youngsters spend time making dainty daisy chains and humble crowns.

Historically linked to Venus, the goddess of love, you can also play 'Love Me, Love Me Not' by picking the petals off one by one to see if your beau really, truly does love you.

BUTTERCUP *Ranunculus acris*
Discover if each person you meet really does like butter or if they're just making it up. Simply hold the flower under their chin; if it reflects yellow, then you have your positive answer.

PURPLE TOADFLAX *Linaria purpurea*
This tall, wispy plant is a hardy perennial and looks stunning arranged in a simple glass milk bottle. It's a sure winner with the local bees and butterflies too.

The name is so given because its tiny flowers resemble a toad's face when you look closely, which small eyes will love to confirm.

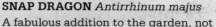

SNAP DRAGON *Antirrhinum majus*
A fabulous addition to the garden, not just because of the stunning array of colours available, but also given they can be so much fun.

Carefully pull a fully formed flower head off of the stalk and squeeze in the middle, making the dragon's jaws snap open and closed.

LOVE IN A MIST *Nigella damascena*
Once introduced to your garden, they are strong self-seeders, so their gloriously peculiar blooms will return year after year.

Sometimes called Ragged Lady, the delicate flowers and hazy foliage are thought to represent wishing for a kiss and that you are open to love.

LILY OF THE VALLEY *Convallaria majalis*
Legend has it that these tiny, jingly bell-shaped flowers symbolize happiness.

In France it is custom to give a small bunch to family and friends on the first of May for good luck, or *bonne chance* in French. Beware, though, they are poisonous if eaten.

CHIVES *Allium schoenoprasum*
Once established, chives are a wonderful plant to snip the tips off of, to be added to your dinner, from stir fries to salads. Their flowers are also edible and taste delicious, making any dish look bright and cheery. They are a good introduction to onions for youngsters.

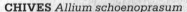
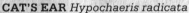

CAT'S EAR *Hypochaeris radicata*
So-called because of its fine-haired leaves. Little eyes will often find tiny black pollen beetles inside amongst the petals and may take great delight in tipping them out and studying them.

Also known as False Dandelion, these square-ended petal blooms grow high and dance joyfully in the breeze, whilst their leaves remain on the ground, giving them another name of Flatweed.

Sewing Project

Sewing is a fundamental life skill. Mending is a useful lesson to teach youngsters – even more so now that we must watch what we discard. Learning to sew is another feather in their cap of independence.

You can use any old scraps of fabric. I don't tend to throw any material away; it all gets stored in an old laundry basket for a rainy day.

INGREDIENTS FOR A MEMORABLE DAY
• Spare fabric or old clothes • Simple sewing kit including scissors, cottons, needles and pins • Needle threader helps younger ones • Sewing machine if your project calls for it • Cardboard or old cereal boxes for templates

---

TRASH INTO TREASURE

The teddy bear shown here was made from a liner of an unwanted Barbour jacket, the black cat from an old tablecloth and the doll from an old dress and top. Check charity shops for fabrics. Old curtains, bedding and even clothes on the bargain rail that have interesting textures or colours can make unique items.

You could even use clothes that your youngsters have grown out of – we have made a duck cuddly from the watercolour print of a duck on an old T-shirt and a cushion from an old starry dress. They make for wonderful memories and T-shirt material is soft enough to cuddle up with at night, so a perfect material to work with.

PROJECT IDEAS

You don't need to restrict yourself to cuddlies though, other projects might include:
• Pin cushions
• Bunting (see page 45 for DIY)
• Pouch for sunglasses
• Pencil cases
• Sleeping eye masks
• Play food
• Patchwork quilt for the eager
• Sleeping bag for a teddy or doll
• Utility belt for an action man
• Cape for a superhero
• Tepee (many thanks to the chickens, Bertha and Margaret, for modelling ours overleaf)
• Tablecloth den (see page 64 for DIY)
• Simple square cushion or a lightning bolt cushion for their bed

SAFETY

Our daughter has been sitting on my lap whilst I have used the sewing machine since she was a baby. Nowadays she competently sews on the machine by pressing the foot pedal by hand on the table, instead of the floor, understanding the dangers involved.

Hand sewing is a better place to start though. A simple cushion and blanket for a teddy for really young ones – straight lines are easy for them to pick up. A simple alien hand puppet is fun and easy to create as they progress.

Just remember safety. Always switch the machine off as soon as you stop using it. Remember to teach them to avoid eyes when using a needle; sewing downwards and pulling the needle away from them helps to eliminate this problem.

And remember, if you are seen to be fixing or mending something instead of buying new, this way of thinking will become second nature for the next generation.

CLEAR AND CLOUDLESS SKY?

I don't recommend sewing in bright sunlight as you are more likely to stab your finger with the needle. However, you can take a simple project such as French knitting with you and hand stitch in the dappled shade. Your creation will have a wonderful memory associated with it.

You could also think of a project for outside, such as a camouflage canopy for the treehouse or quilting a cheery cover on to an unused single duvet for a soft outdoor playmat. Maybe create a dry fishing game by sewing keyring hoops on to felt fish, using hooks attached to string and a cane, perfect for developing hand–eye coordination and fine motor skills. All kinds of free patterns and ideas can be found online.

Tablecloth Playhouse

This has been a real hit with all ages. In fact, a rather lazy, forty-something, family member claims that this is the best place he has ever had a nap. And it was very easy to make without any difficult sewing techniques. It's a perfect spot for snacks or pudding, such as brownies (recipe on page 65).

INGREDIENTS FOR A MEMORABLE DAY
- Tablecloth playhouse (DIY overleaf) • Small mattress, pillow and blanket
- Play food • Folding tray table • Rechargeable light • Toys and games

---

SETTING UP

Table dens are ideal for a small home, where you may not be able to fit in a tent or a playhouse for youngsters to hide themselves away in. Being made entirely of fabric means it is easily stored when not in use.

You could always make it out of cotton sheets and leave the sides unsewn, so that it can still be used as a tablecloth which you can pop your knees under when seated at the table, and with the added bonus of being able to machine wash it.

FOR SNOOZE AND PLAY

This secret space is ideal for naps, and I'm not just talking about young ones or the aforementioned fully grown fella, but the dog too. We all know where Dex is when this novelty tablecloth comes out.

To help make it homely inside, we use our daughter's old crib mattress with a pillow and blanket for a bed. I've made a mini stove top on a storage box, which holds small metal pans and some play food. She uses our rechargeable emergency light inside and moves her cuddlies in.

CLEAR AND CLOUDLESS SKY?

If you have wide patio doors or a balcony, why not take the table outside in sunny weather for novelty value? Whilst it is out there, set up table tennis on the top before you bring it back in.

And then, as the sun goes down, have a disco in the space left behind indoors (see page 32). There will be more room to throw some of your legendary moves.

Making a Tablecloth Playhouse

YOU WILL NEED

• Old or inexpensive blankets or sheets • Felt for the windows and flowers • Voile or similar for the curtains • Ribbon for the curtain ties • Cotton threads and sewing kit • Sewing machine – optional but makes this much quicker to stitch

1. This den was created out of inexpensive blankets. I used two blankets for the roof, which I sewed together first. Then I draped it over the table, with a heavy pot in the middle to keep it in place as I worked. I then used two more blankets for the sides. I pinned the side blankets to the roof blankets and cut off the excess fabric, folding and pinning the corners in as I went. I then sewed around the top of the side blankets attaching them to the roof blankets with a simple straight stitch on the machine, leaving a gap for the door.

2. The door was cut to size from a scrap of fabric and hemmed all the way around. If you wish to add a door number and a felt wreath, do that now; it will be a little tricky to do later. Next, I pinned the door under the roof so that it hangs only from the top. Sew into position on the machine.

3. Next, I cut two squares of white felt for the windows. Then I cut a piece of paper to the same size for each window. On each piece of paper, draw four small squares which will be cut out as the openings for the windows – but not just yet! Pin both felt windows with the paper over the top, in place either side of the door.

Now sew around the outside of the square, stitching the paper and felt into place (you will remove the paper later). Then sew around each of the smaller squares that you have drawn. Next, using sharp scissors, carefully cut out each of the four small squares. Make sure to stay inside your stitching and be careful not to snip where you have sewn. The paper may now be torn off and discarded. You will be left with four holes to look out of. Repeat for your second window.

4. Finally, I cut voile fabric to size for curtains. Whilst the den was in place, I handstitched the voile fabric inside along the top. I included two short lengths of ribbon stitched to the side blankets to tie the curtains back with. If you wish, you can adorn the front with silk or felt flowers.

CHOCOLATE COURGETTE BROWNIES

This recipe is a really nice change to using courgettes in savoury dishes, where they tend to absorb other flavours very well. The courgettes here make the brownies deliciously moist; however, this does mean they won't last long in a tin. Oh no, what a shame. Guess you will have to eat them all today then.

MAKES 16

Ingredients

- 150g (1¼ cups) plain flour
- 150g butter (¾ cup) (or replace butter and eggs for 300g (1 cup) apple purée for vegan version)
- 50g (½ cup) cacao or cocoa powder
- 2 tsp baking powder
- ½ tsp salt
- 100g (½ cup) sugar (or your chosen sweetener equivalent)
- 3 eggs
- 1 tsp vanilla essence
- 2 courgettes, grated (around 300g (10oz))
- 100g (½ cup) chocolate chips (milk or dark chocolate chips both work well)

Directions

1. Preheat oven to 180°C / Fan 160°C / Gas 4 / 350°F

2. Put all the ingredients except the courgette and chocolate chips into a bowl and mix well. Use an electric mixer to introduce lots of air to make them light.

3. Add in grated courgette and chocolate chips and mix by hand until everything is combined.

4. Grease a square tin or ovenproof dish with butter and pour in your mixture, spreading it evenly across the top.

5. Pop in the oven for 50–60 minutes, until a skewer comes out clean.

6. Portion into squares and allow to cool on a wire rack whilst you wait patiently.

Oh, my goodness, these are so moreish. Therefore, if you find yourself unable to leave them alone, they also freeze very well. Simply defrost within three months; if you wish you can heat for 30 seconds in a microwave to warm them up, and add lashings, I mean a moderate amount, of cream.

Shoebox Mouse House

On the rare occasion that we come by a shoebox, we keep it safely tucked away until a day when we might be stuck indoors – they make wonderful miniature houses that you can pack everything back into and store away safely.

INGREDIENTS FOR A MEMORABLE DAY
• Shoebox • Old remnants of ribbon and fabric • Small items that could make something special (see list on page 69) • Scissors • PVA glue and glue gun • Tape • Natural treasures such as dried wheat sheaths and woodland nuts for food for the mouse • Shells, twigs and dried flowers

---

SETTING UP

The beauty of making a mouse house is that it captivates the imagination of youngsters and elders alike. Boring little items now become treasure for a little mouse looking to decorate his new abode.

If you loved the tales of *The Borrowers*, then I am certain that you will take great delight in creating a small world for a tiny creature that sees things differently.

SAVING TREASURES

If you know you might want to make a house, simply start a collection in advance and save any small, discarded items that might be destined for the rubbish bin – loose sequins, a remnant of ribbon, bottle tops, corks, dried flowers. It will all come in handy.

OLDER CHILDREN

For older children, perhaps suggest they make a miniature version of their bedroom or maybe a camouflaged camp for an action hero.

Shoebox houses are wonderful as they last longer than usual arts and crafts. Your family will now be on the lookout for little treasures to add to it, revitalizing play and continuing the fun.

When you are out on a walk, keep an eye out for small natural treasures such as nuts, sticks, pebbles, seed heads, bark, feathers, pinecones, lichen. Put them somewhere safe for a rainy day and mouse house building.

IDEAS FOR FURNISHINGS

Miniature furniture and shoe box home decorations can be made from all kinds of things including:

- Cotton reels as tables
- Cut down corks as seats
- Prosecco metal bottle caps turned into elaborate chairs
- Match boxes stacked and taped or glued together to make drawers
- Plastic laundry scoops as sinks
- Yoghurt pots as baths
- Lolly stick ladders
- Chocolate box beds
- Fabric remnant rugs and blankets
- Foil pans, taps and mirrors
- Toilet roll stoves with sticks inside and a tissue paper fire
- Small pegs to fix paintings on the wall
- Pompom beanbags
- Buttons as plates
- Acorn sheaths for cups
- Cockle shells for bowls
- Dried flowers in miniature glitter jar vases
- Miniature tepee from scrap fabric and kebab sticks
- Pizza box tripods as tables
- Scenes cut from magazines, placed behind lolly stick window frames
- Different shaped beads as toys, all stored away neatly in little tiny jam jars sneaked out of a hotel after breakfast time

CLEAR AND CLOUDLESS SKY?

Take the box outside if the weather is kind. Make a mouse house for a real mouse (although maybe discourage leaving real food in there as real mice can be quite pesky). Use straw on the floor, a twig wigwam adorned with leaves and flowers for a bedroom.

Use a horse chestnut husk to make a sink for water. A sturdy, fragrant bay leaf makes a decadent tray and empty acorn cups or shells for bowls. It's amazing what natural treasures can be converted into for a little mouse to enjoy.

Picnic in the Sunshine

You might think our family's world revolves around meals. And you would be right. Picnics, I believe, nurture the soul. Eating meals outside just makes everything taste a little bit better. The accompanying bird song makes things feel more real and alive – and dappled sunlight is always welcome.

INGREDIENTS FOR A MEMORABLE DAY
- Blanket • Chopping board table • Basket or crate for carrying your picnic
- Drinks and glasses • Playing cards • Poetry books • Blanket and pegs for den
- Umbrella or canes and a sheet for shelter

LOCATION

We eat outdoors whenever we can – we picnic in the woods, the park, have early morning breakfast at the beach with the gas stove, take our baguettes beside the river, enjoy lazy afternoon tea in a meadow, eat our salads on the sand out of glass jars, a picnic tea at the allotment – whenever, wherever we can.

A simple backpack or a strong basket and a thermos or water bottle is all the equipment you really need. You do not need anything fancy to pack a light meal.

However, I can recommend a crate for a table, a small wooden chopping board for cutting bread and to provide a level surface for drinks, cloth napkins which can be used as plates and a woollen blanket if you are willing to carry them. A corkscrew is not to be frowned upon for adults partaking.

SETTING UP

The truth is though, you do not need to venture far for a truly decadent picnic. Simply step into the garden or park. For real comfort carry out the blankets, eiderdowns and cushions.

Branches of a tree may offer shade; if not, pop the garden umbrella up. Or simply wrangle four canes into the ground, and top with a flat sheet tied at each corner to a cane, for an easy fix if the sun is too strong. Tray tables are very useful, or an upside-down crate works well.

A cheery vase of flowers can be collected by the youngsters: give them a jam jar each and tell them which flowers are out of bounds. Encourage the children to make daisy chains and dandelion crowns whilst you set up.

FOOD

Picnics can be as simple or as elaborate as you like. A simple loaf of crusty bread, in-season tomatoes and a cheese of your choice. Serve with fruit – chunks of watermelon, orange slices, strawberries and cherries make excellent puddings. Berries with croissants and pastries make a delicious breakfast. Or simply make pesto outside to accompany a fresh loaf (see opposite), picking and using herbs growing in your own garden.

Or go all out for a special occasion. Meze platters, stuffed baguettes, cheese and biscuits with grapes, cheese scones slathered in butter, olives, stuffed peppers, wraps, rice balls, pizza slices – all of which can be prepared by you and the youngsters together earlier in the day. Add carrot sticks, cucumber slices, freshly harvested peas still in their pods and baby corn on the side.

Platters with a variety of food to share work well in encouraging younger ones to try new things. Or if you are feeling brave, allow the youngsters to choose the menu.

LATER ON

Grab a poetry book and a pack of cards for afterwards. Lean a tall stick against a tree and throw a pegged blanket over for a makeshift den whilst you enjoy a cheeky glass of wine in the sunshine.

TOP TIPS

My own parents always made a big deal about meals; we would all eat together and discuss each other's days. We have ensured that we instil those values in our own daughter. Mealtimes together really are the most treasured part of each day.

If you have trouble keeping younger ones at the table (or blanket), try playing 'Best, Worst, Funniest', where you take it in turns to name the best, worst and funniest moments of your day. This also helps extract crucial information from children of school age. Be sure to listen to their answers though. A friend once told me, if you do not listen to the little things, they may not tell you the big stuff later on.

OVERCAST?

Moving inside can sometimes be even more fun because of the unexpected element. Let the youngsters decide where to set up the picnic blanket. Later, once the young ones have headed off to bed, leave the picnic blanket there, dim the lights, light a candle and enjoy the romance with an Irish coffee and chocolates.

MINTY PESTO

This is a lovely recipe, which is fun to make, easy to throw together and full of healthy ingredients. Encouraging children to have fun with making their own food will mean they are more likely to try new flavours and perhaps eat a few more nutrients without even noticing. We have made this pesto in the kitchen, in the garden and in the middle of a field while camping. It's a real crowd pleaser.

Experiment with other nuts such as macadamia and walnuts. You can omit nuts altogether and replace with seeds like sunflower and flax seed.

Keep a potted herb garden near your back door and throw in whatever you have an abundance of – coriander, parsley and chives all work well with this.

Ingredients

Quantities can be amended according to taste, however as a rough guide:

- Generous handful of fresh mint leaves
- Handful of fresh basil leaves
- Pinch of smoked salt
- Splash of garlic infused olive oil
- Handful of cashew nuts
- Two handfuls of pistachios (shelled)
- Two handfuls of fresh peas or frozen petit pois

Directions

1. Tear up the fresh herbs and place in a pestle and mortar (or blender) with a little smoked salt. The salt will help to crush the herb leaves nicely.

2. Once they have had a good bash, throw in the nuts along with a glug of the oil and continue crushing with the pestle.

3. Scrape your mixture off the sides. It should be smelling ridiculously delicious by now.

4. Steam or boil your petit pois until ready to eat. Then add them to the mix, crush again and combine together.

5. Serve immediately on sliced fresh bread.

Brilliant Boxes

Although I adore little worlds you don't always need to think small for creating something out of boxes. Whenever we get a large delivery, there is much excitement for our next project. If you don't have anywhere to store a large box, you could always flat pack it and slide it under a bed or behind a wardrobe until you have the time to create.

INGREDIENTS FOR A MEMORABLE DAY
• Boxes – large and small • Tape • Sticks and duct tape to reinforce and support
• Scissors • Paint, pens or crayons to decorate • Any other recycled objects for dolls' house furniture or buttons or handles

---

GO BIG

We have a winter ritual whereby we save any large boxes and, come November, we make a large creation that can stay up until Christmas. This large dolls' house was one of our projects. However, my favourite was a ginormous space station, covered in foil with knobs and buttons made from saved milk caps and coffee jar lids. It was truly out of this world!

You could turn a discarded giant box into a weather station, a spaceship, a tank, a car, a kitchen, a television, a cottage, a castle, a bed, a cave. An ongoing project, like our space station, meant the family could add to it whenever we had the time. Equally, youngsters can be left to decorate it as they see fit.

THINK LONGEVITY

I always try to encourage a project that will last a few weeks, so that we get the most out of it. Once you lose the rigidity of the box, play can often become impossible. Therefore, if necessary, reinforce the cardboard with tape, glue or sticks, to ensure that play continues for much longer.

A space station may last a few weeks whilst they are obsessing over deep space exploration. Or a fairy castle might last a while provided you add one or two supports to accommodate the footfall of the Barbie posse.

BUILDING WITH BOXES

With a little planning, you can create something quite exciting. Why stop at one cardboard cottage when you could open a whole village (provided you don't mind losing the dining room for a few days!) with a market stall, a vet clinic and a post office. Mention to friends and family that you're planning a project and they may save their large boxes for you too.

BE SURE TO RECYCLE

Just remember to recycle your projects when the time comes. One of the reasons we build our box project in late autumn, when the weather is usually pretty shocking, is because this is a great pastime for indoors, but also we are able to give our daughter the head's up that come Christmas it has to go. That way there is little upset on the day, as we're usually replacing it with a Christmas tree. She helps to dismantle it and save her favourite pieces, like any dolls' house furniture that can continue to be used.

CLEAR AND CLOUDLESS SKY?

During the warmer months, you can move your box building outside. Cut holes for a door and a window into a large cardboard box, and leaving the box plain, place it in the centre of the lawn (garden umbrella up if it's hot and sunny). Now leave the poster paints out and allow your family to decorate it all over.

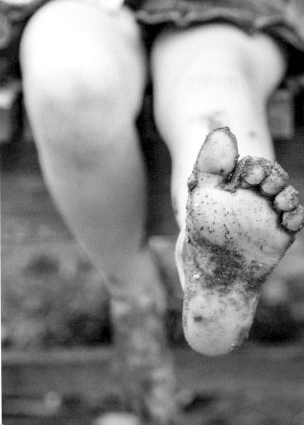

Obstacle Course

Obstacle courses are so much fun and can keep the family amused for ages. Make it adult friendly and you can get lost in an afternoon of trying to beat each other's best time to complete the course, which can be brilliant exercise if you have a competitive streak.

INGREDIENTS FOR A MEMORABLE DAY
• Chairs • Low tables • Blankets • Tunnels • Play equipment • Steps • Rugs
• Hula hoops • Sports equipment • Stopwatch • Scoreboard/chalk board to record scores

---

SETTING UP

When it comes to creating the perfect obstacle course, anything goes. Think items to climb over, wriggle through, balance on, clamber over, walk along or jump from (safety permitting).

We tend to place our obstacles in a circle, but if you have a big enough space, why not snake it around the garden, incorporating what is already in place such as swings, slides, steps to jump from, trees to run around, garden tables to crawl under.

OBSTACLE IDEAS

Some easy obstacles to cobble together could include:
- Plank of wood to walk across
- Hula hoops to jump through or hula with
- Soft archery set or water pistol with a paper target
- Skipping rope strung across two chairs to limbo under
- Pop up tunnels
- Play equipment like a mini slide, a trampoline or a balance board
- Kitchen steps to clamber up or jump from
- Table with a cloth over to crawl under
- Chalk line to 'tightrope walk' along
- Swimming noodles pegged in the ground to crawl through
- Any chairs or coffee tables that might be a bit of a squeeze to crawl under
- Beanbags to throw into a box or a hula hoop
- Thick logs as balance beams
- Tyres to jump in and out of
- Cones to weave in and out of
- Ladders laid down flat to jump through the rungs

PLAN AHEAD

Take a stroll through your home and garden to spot any obvious pieces of furniture you could drag out. Do you have a thickset rug that you could take outside to make a softer mat for forward rolls?

Do you have a couple of tall breakfast bar chairs which could be draped with a blanket for a tunnel that might accommodate an adult?

Do you have a few stored paving slabs or sturdy leftover tiles you could use as stepping stones? Have a rummage and see what you can find. Make it as easy or as epic as you like, but keep it safe and age appropriate.

MIX IT UP

If the only coffee table you own is built for a small one to crawl under, don't expect the grown-ups to compete fairly – the inevitable moment when somebody gets stuck usually means your children have vanished to grab a camera. Change that obstacle to something else such as three press-ups on the side of the table for a grown-up.

Are you throwing beanbags into a hula hoop? Mark out a smaller circle with a piece of rope and make it harder for the grown-ups. No cheating!

OVERCAST?

If you are lucky enough to have a hallway, even a skinny one like ours, you can cram a long line of obstacles into a small space. It's double the fun because once you reach the end, you have to then come back the other way!

Or simply utilize your whole house. Set up different obstacles in each room; think crawling under or behind the dining table or chairs, rolling across the bed, jumping off the bottom step of the stairs. But beware, you may need an adjudicator to ensure there is no foul play!

SUN WATER

This is great fun to make in the spring, just as the sun starts to show itself again. You can make sun water from the first of the strawberries, maybe even picked from your own garden. You could even start growing strawberries and mint to ensure a steady stream of sun water, allowing the youngsters to assemble it themselves.

Cucumber or lemon also make colourful drinks but are not as sweet. Blueberries look fun and are fab for nibbling on (be mindful that they can be a choking hazard to young tots), but they don't tend to flavour the water as much if left whole.

Sun water is so simple and particularly fun for toddlers.

MAKES ONE JAR

Ingredients

- Strawberries
- Oranges
- Mint leaves
- Water

Directions

1. Grab a jar with a lid and add slices of strawberries and orange. Poke in a few mint leaves too and top up with fresh water.
2. Give the jar a little shake and place in the sunshine, shaking periodically and sip once warmed through.

Best to drink sun water by the end of the day, so it does not spoil. Or leave it in the fridge for later, allowing time for the flavours to mingle.

Build a Den

There's no better way to spend a morning than building a den or bower and then spending the rest of the day relaxing inside. Your den can be a mighty blanket fort from which to launch epic battles or a dainty bower fit for a queen. If you have enough sheets and blankets a truly worthwhile den can, if you let it, take over your garden. Challenge accepted, I see you nodding.

INGREDIENTS FOR A MEMORABLE DAY
• Blankets and sheets and tablecloths and large scarves • Pegs (metal, flexi-grip or sturdy bamboo are best) • Cushions and pillows

---

SIZE DOESN'T MATTER
Despite the above challenge, you don't need to let it get out of control. A simple den under a bush provides much hilarity to smaller folk as they watch their parents attempt to clamber in and out. You don't need much space to make a fort, just enough room to all huddle up to read a book or enjoy snacks together.

We often use this bed canopy outside for a simple open-fronted den, which can easily be made to feel cosy, and even double up with keeping the mosquitoes out after sunset! However, you can of course . . .

GO LARGE
Once we had a free day, so naturally we thought ginormous den. We raided the linen cupboard for spare sheets, blankets, tablecloths and random pieces of fabric that I have collected over the years specifically for occasions such as these. The monumental tablecloth I found on the pound rail at a charity shop years ago was put to good use.

We *did* go large. We lost the back garden. At times, we didn't even know which way was up, it was temporarily disconcerting. But we found each other and installed better pegging. Note – don't bother with traditional wooden pegs, they're not much use. For the structural sides, you need the flexi-grip or metal pegs – bring out the bad boys.

If you're getting really serious, invite friends over and tell them to bring their spare flat sheets and tablecloths too. See how far you can go with den building. Push those boundaries!

SETTING UP

We used the garden umbrella in its heavily weighted base and our stepladders to add height. Using some old remnants of fabric that we didn't mind making holes in, we tied them off safely. We used plant pots and bricks to weigh down the edges along the outside. It might be worth checking the weather forecast; if high winds are due imminently, abort.

FURNISHING INSIDE

For a tented den of this magnitude, we went with luxury and dragged a few rugs outside. The garden furniture was moved inside. We even added an old foam mattress and a blanket for naps. Once you've come this far, why not go the whole way with style and comfort. Decorate as you wish.

WHAT NOW?

Kick back and relax. Play games, read books and mags, eat ALL of your meals out there. Is it a warm evening? It would be silly not to grab the airbed and the sleeping bags. We built our fort around our play shed which houses the 'Funky Chicken' restaurant, so we had a constant supply of salt dough bananas and glasses of 'wine' on tap. Eventually, the real wine made an appearance.

Provided there is little wind forecast overnight, don't take it down straight away. See page 85 for ideas for what you could do the following day.

OVERCAST?

Overcast does not mean game over. It's actually quite cosy being nestled inside a den on a gloomy day, just remember to stay warm.

However, rain and wind might blight your plans. There's no harm in taking in it indoors, though. Perhaps see how far you can get – can you build a blanket fort that covers two rooms? Three? Congrats, that's epic. You should be proud. If you can link the whole of your downstairs, I want to see pictures!

Bird Watching

You have made your epic den (see page 81) and it has taken over the garden to the extent that you do not know where anything is anymore, and it's the morning after and your young folk have moved on to something else, but you cannot bear to tear it down. What do you do? Have a bird watching day! I am not kidding when I tell you that we spent another six hours out there, bird watching. It was the most peaceful, relaxing day I can remember. Of course, you can do this without having built a tent fort too.

INGREDIENTS FOR A MEMORABLE DAY
• Den or hide • Rugs, blankets, cushions • Bird feed • Cameras • Pens, pencils and paper • Books and magazines • Nature guides to help identify feathered friends • Snacks

---

TWITCHING IS THE ANSWER

We filled up the bird feeders and topped up the bird bath and retired into the tent to make little gaps in the sheets for the cameras to peep through. The quickest camera was set up on a tripod and others were placed on low tables and chairs, with spare batteries at the ready.

The trick is to make it cosy in the den (or some place to sit quietly if you haven't built a den), with rugs, blankets, cushions and throws. However, given we had to be quiet and stay still long enough to allow the birds to feel safe to visit, this presented a challenge for a tiny naturalist. But not for long.

I found all the low tables and crates we had in the house and swept up all the favourite books to read, paper, colouring books and pens, nature spotter's books and magazines, and of course non-rustling snacks, and deposited them inside the den, now a converted twitcher's hide.

It was a wonderful day which taught all of us a great deal about slowing down, enjoying the moment, as well as a few new photography skills.

KEEP A LIST

Encourage the youngsters to jot down what they have seen, even sketching them (you too), noting key features. Why not get the watercolour paints out to add a little flourish to each drawing?

Waiting quietly is also an opportunity to have a bash at improvised poetry writing or perhaps try a haiku structure for fun (three lines of poetry – the first line must be five syllables, the second line seven syllables, the third line five syllables).

It can be a real thrill to share photographs after each visitor has been. We knew that between 3 p.m. and 4 p.m. tends to be their teatime, so once they had finished feasting we ended on a high.

There are wonderful apps available that allow you to record birdsong and it will identify which bird is serenading you.

WHAT TO LOOK OUT FOR

Depending on the time of year, you may get blackbirds (always smart looking), robins (very proud), sparrows (our humble friends), thrushes (a very special sight), dunnocks (with their hilarious mating ritual!), starlings (so suave), collared doves (oh, the romance), greenfinches (always jovial), goldfinches (just wow), blue tits (that glorious colour), wagtails (perpetually cheery chaps) and great tits (dressed ready for the ball) stopping by in your garden (see pages 88–9 for a few).

We were lucky enough to have a teeny, tiny wren pause for a photo. And as we packed away, the whole family appeared in the bush alongside, and then they were gone!

FOOD MATTERS

Obviously good snacks for you are important. But that's not what I mean. I mean for the birdies. Plan a little in advance if you can and around two to four weeks before your bird-watching day, try encouraging different breeds to feed in your garden. This will ensure plenty of visitors – and some great shots on the day.

Think small seed (like millet) for sparrows, dunnocks and finches. Tits love sunflower seeds, but the striped sunflower seed is tough to crack open, so black sunflower seed might be best. Pigeons and doves will thank you for wheat and barley. Pinhead oatmeal is a crowd pleaser, especially with robins and goldfinches. Thrushes might be interested in a few raisins. You might be able to entice a nuthatch or a woodpecker with peanuts, but they must be in a feeder as small birdies might choke on them whole.

OVERCAST?

There's no need to worry if the sky looks heavy; simply move inside and find a window spot. This might mean moving a bit of furniture, or even placing a couple of chairs near the window to get cosy. You can still have great fun watching for hungry and thirsty visitors.

Garden Birds

ROBIN *Erithacus rubecula*
Often a constant companion in the
garden, robins are always a welcome sight
throughout the winter months, their cheery
red breast adding a splash of colour when
much of the garden has been put to bed.

GOLDFINCH *Carduelis carduelis*
To spot one in your garden truly is a sight,
but to watch it take flight is something else.
Their long line of yellow across their wings is
so cheery. I can see why they are thought to
symbolize joy and optimism.

DUNNOCK *Prunella modularis*
These cute little creatures are often
seen feeding in pairs; I like the
romance of them. Often dismissed
as a sparrow, their nickname is
actually hedge sparrow.

WREN *Troglodytes troglodytes*
The second smallest of the UK's birds (goldcrest wins),
the mouse-like wren is said to symbolize enthusiasm for
life. With their birdcall being quite loud for their size, I
can believe it.

CHAFFINCH *Fringilla coelebs*
Sporting a fancy outfit, chaffinches have a loud song, and have been found to have regional accents, depending on where they live!

HOUSE SPARROW
Passer domesticus
The humble house sparrows are like old friends in our garden. Always reliably appearing at 3 p.m. for tea, they sit chattering happily in groups, accompanying our afternoons outdoors.

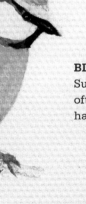

BLUE TIT *Cyanistes caeruleus*
Such a welcome little lot, these colourful birds can often be seen pinching bits of door mat and dog hair (they're welcome to it!) to line their nests.

GREAT TIT *Parus major*
I always think they look like they are dressed for the ball in their tuxedos and black caps. Larger than the blue tits, they come to feed dressed in their best.

Wildlife Hunting

This is not just an activity for curious pre-schoolers. Spend some time in your garden, seeking out and identifying your local insect community. Figure out what furry and feathered creatures reside in your shaded nooks and crannies. What is in that dropping over there? Can you see tiny bones in it? Maybe you have an owl. Are you growing night phlox? Chances are you will see plenty of moths once the sun goes down. And guess what? That means bats too! Become a detective in your own backyard.

INGREDIENTS FOR A MEMORABLE DAY
• Pen and paper • Nature guide for identification • Logs, sticks, leaves and string for building homes • Camera • Clear pot or jar and magnifying glass

---

CREATE A HAVEN
This is an easy way to get the whole family involved. Sort out the architects and engineers in your clan, inspire your builders and interior designers, and create a home fit for a two, four, six, eight or even one hundred-legged creature!

Make a bug house from logs and stones. Create a spider's spot by twining sticks together and leaving near a doorway, where flies are guaranteed to whizz past. Build a nest box from scraps of wood. Make hanging bird feeders (see page 93 for a DIY) to attract a few feathered friends.

Upturned plant pots in a shaded nook with rotting leaves is a perfect home for a frog or toad; leave a shallow basin of water nearby too. Sow some wildflowers to attract bees and even offer them a spot to hide away over the winter by twining a few sticks of bamboo together. Create a shallow pond for newts to wallow, a compost for worms, a rockery in a sunny spot for lizards, a leafy den for hedgehogs to burrow into.

CHECK IT REGULARLY
Create a journal of what you find and where. See if the shaded, darker, colder areas are preferred by some and discover who likes the sunny, open areas. Check back every now and then and you may find different species throughout the year.

Have you ever seen how ladybirds transform? Several years ago, I brought a cabbage leaf home from the allotment and placed it in a habitat indoors, thinking we might be lucky enough to hatch some cabbage white butterflies. When they opened into crazy little armoured insects, I was a little surprised. However, we researched it and allowed them to stay and sure enough, they turned into chrysalids and later hatched out again, but this time into beautiful ladybirds.

BE KIND

If you do disturb the wildlife, teach the youngsters to be kind and responsible and pop those worms back in the mud or let the woodlice retreat behind the logs. And should you be lucky enough to find a bird's nest, be sure to leave it where it is until nesting season has completely finished. Should you find a hibernating creature, thank them for making a home in your garden and leave them to sleep on.

OTHER ACTIVITIES

Your hunt around the garden can inspire other fun ideas, such as painting butterflies, making wings from wire coat hangers and old tights, making a chrysalid from a duvet ready for a story.

Perhaps research which flowers and trees attract which species and plan a few additions to your garden. Set up a tray of damp sand overnight with tempting morsels of food nearby to see if you can catch any tracks to identify who might be out at night. Plan a bat watching evening, snuggled under a blanket on the lawn at dusk (see page 37 for some star-gazing tips).

You will never be sorry you embraced nature and encouraged your family to learn more about who and what shares the space around you.

OVERCAST?

It's an opportunity! You might find out something new. For example, blackbirds will tap the ground for worms in the rain as the worms come higher to the surface when it rains. We enjoyed watching a daddy blackbird try to teach his offspring how to do it, it was hilarious. The youngster thought that tapping the decking might do the trick. Hopefully he learned quickly.

Frogs and toads will venture out to eat in the rain, as will pesky slugs. I certainly don't mind them not being returned to my veg patch.

BIRD FEEDER

There's no need to throw your orange peel away when you can make a few of these bird feeders and dot them around the garden, encouraging your feathered friends to join you for their tea.

When fruit is scarce in the winter months, throw in a handful of raisins or sultanas as a little sweet treat to make the chilly days cheery for your newfound friends. Your garden will become known as the place to go for the best grub.

MAKES 4 FEEDERS

Ingredients

- Two whole oranges
- Eight 60cm (24in) lengths of string or twine
- 150g (1 cup) of wild bird seed
- 50g (½ cup) oats
- 50g (½ cup) vegetable suet

Directions

1. Cut your oranges in half and scoop out the flesh with a teaspoon. Eat the flesh now for a snack or add to your porridge in the morning.

2. Thread a large-eyed needle with twine or string. Make two holes in line with each other in the top of the orange peel half. Thread the twine through. Repeat with another length of string and two more holes opposite the first, creating two large loops to hang it with. Knot to secure in place.

3. Melt the suet in a pan. Remove from the heat and add the bird seed and oats, mixing thoroughly.

4. Scoop the mixture, whilst still warm, into the empty orange halves and allow to cool completely before hanging them in the garden. Twenty minutes in the fridge will do it.

Bushcraft Day

You don't need to live near any woods, you can create a bushcraft day at home. Spend the whole day outside and live off the land – you're only allowed in for the lavatory! Unless you keep chickens, then maybe wee around the chicken run to deter foxes. Just putting that out there.

INGREDIENTS FOR A MEMORABLE DAY
• Items for den building such as blankets, cushions, etc. • Backpack with magnifying glass and binoculars • Elastic bands, scissors, a knife (just for you to cut twigs, etc.) and string • Nature identification guidebooks • Baskets and containers
• Garden games such as archery or lawn darts

HAVE FUN DISCOVERING

You can incorporate a wildlife hunt (see page 90) and discover what creatures live in your garden. Have a look at what trees you have growing nearby (see pages 142–3 for a few to spot). Take a moment to identify the flowers in your garden (see pages 56–7 for some). Perhaps make a hide out of an old tablecloth to do a spot of bird watching (see page 84).

Fill a backpack with binoculars, a nature identifier book, bug box, magnifying glass, paper and pen. Encourage the youngsters to use the book themselves to search for that violet shimmering beetle, or that hovering moth-like looking creature with a long nose. Showing them how to research themselves is empowering.

GET CRAFTING

For younger ones you could make a nature wand or a memory stick: find a stick and twist elastic bands all the way up. Then, as you walk around, pop anything interesting you find under the elastic band, thereby creating a beautiful keepsake. Include leaves, flowers, feathers, grasses, seeds; we even had a dead hoverfly in there once.

For the older children, if you are lucky enough to have a large tree in your garden which drops bits of wood, have a go at making something: perhaps roping a few twigs together to make a tray, or sawing up an apple tree log to make 'plates' to present your dinner. Maybe, if you think the neighbours are safely out of range, make slingshots!

Perhaps have a go at garden archery (family kits include arrows with suckers on the end so that all ages can have a go). We made some rudimentary bows from a bendy willow twig and string and popped some pigeon feathers in the end of a split twig for an arrow. They were completely ineffective, but fun to make!

Collect fallen twigs for firewood for later that evening. Perhaps even forage for your dinner. Do you have a blackberry bush in the garden? That's pudding sorted (if they are ripe). Or even some dandelions? The leaves can be cooked like spinach and the yellow petals can be thrown into a salad. Pretty violas are edible and look lovely on a dessert.

Scavenger hunts are fun no matter what your age (see page 127 for ideas), especially when there's the lure of a chocolate prize at the end, teamed with a timer ticking down. You could make some sun water too (recipe on page 79), as it's wonderfully refreshing on a warm day.

BUILD A DEN

It doesn't need to be fancy: a simple camp under a tree or a bush to call home is a wonderful retreat to count seed pods or plan the next major treehouse build. Throw a few comfy cushions down. Remember to provide a few baskets and containers for collecting natural treasures.

Decorate the camp with anything you have found – string twigs together for a mobile. Make an outline with stones to create a magic boundary that must not be crossed without a password.

When you are out and about encourage youngsters to always ask first about picking flowers as some are poisonous and others may be protected. But if you're happy for them to pick a few blooms, mix with a little foliage and make a posy for the camp HQ.

AS THE SUN GOES DOWN

Hang up a white sheet or towel on your washing line and rig up a light nearby to attract a few moths to study – if you're lucky you might have a visit from an elephant hawk-moth with its fancy pink wings.

Seeing as you've spent the day outside, you might as well make a night of it! Camp outside (see page 119 for ideas), cook on the open fire (see page 26), star gaze (see page 37 to get you started), certainly make some dough sticks over the fire (see recipe opposite).

OVERCAST?

If skies start to darken with brooding clouds, take this opportunity to nip to the garage and retrieve a tarp and see if the family can create a shelter from the storm. Maybe that's your cue for hot chocolate (see recipe on page 21) and marshmallows.

If it really is pouring, perhaps try leaf rubbing inside for the youngsters. Or miniature wigwam building with collected twigs and leaves, fit for a fairy. Older children might like to have a go at whittling wood, provided you have the correct equipment and are prepared to supervise.

DOUGH STICKS

These can be sweet or savoury. Make savoury dough sticks by adding either a handful of chopped herbs, or a small handful of chopped sun-dried tomatoes, or even green or black olives chopped finely.

If you have a sweet tooth, dip in chocolate spread. Or keep it simple, leave them plain and coat with a little butter.

Make the dough an hour before you light the fire.

MAKES 8 STICKS

Ingredients

- 1 heaped teaspoon of dried yeast
- ½ tsp sugar
- 200ml (1 cup) warm water (not hot)
- 1 tsp olive oil
- 300g (2 cups) plain flour

Directions

1. Mix the yeast and sugar with the warm water until completely dissolved. Add the oil.
2. Add a little of the flour at a time and mix thoroughly to form a dough.
3. If you are making savoury dough sticks, add any ingredients at this stage. For plain, skip this step.
4. With floured hands, knead the dough for 3–5 minutes and leave to rise for an hour or two, until doubled in size.
5. When you are ready to bake over the fire, split the dough into 8 pieces and making a long, thin sausage, wrap the dough around a stick (bendy sticks work well as you can stake them in the ground, but I like a bamboo cane cut down).
6. Bake over the embers of the fire until golden brown; be careful though – they will be hot!

Family Heritage

One of the sad things about growing up is that by the time we take a real interest in our roots, the elder generation may be gone from our world. As parents, we feel it is vital to engage the younger folk in our family's rich and colourful history, passing on the stories that made us laugh as children. What better way to capture that than in a treasured keepsake book, which can be added to and passed on to the next generation.

INGREDIENTS FOR A MEMORABLE DAY
• Detective hat and magnifying glass optional but good fun • Notepad and pen
• A voice recorder can be useful (there's often one on your phone) • Photos of relatives • Newspaper clippings and invitations, etc. • Scrapbook

---

PLAY DETECTIVE

You can make this into a game. Tell your children that they are all going to be detectives assigned to an important case: how they came to be.

Interview everyone from grandparents to distant cousins. Everybody has a story to tell and may even remember stories from relatives no longer with us that need to be told. And I bet you, everyone you speak to will have some old photographs that they will love to dig out, showing off their adventures, old homes and baby pictures. Think of the treasures you will find.

DETAILS YOU COULD INCLUDE

You can keep a simple photo album, making copies of what you find (I take photos of their photos). You could add a little detail too, written accounts of events or exceptional days. Here's some ideas to include:

• Funny stories
• Where did they come from?
• Special anecdotes like Great Grandfather Abdul spoke 12 different languages or Auntie Mavis used to take in homeless donkeys.
• What was life like growing up? How different is it to now?
• Who did they marry? Can they remember how they first met?
• Can they describe their wedding day? Did anybody make a fool of themselves on the dancefloor? Did anyone fall asleep? There's always one.
• Did they receive any special gifts? During the Second World War, a cabbage or cauliflower was not an uncommon gift.
• What pets did they have?
• How many different jobs did they have? What was their favourite one?

- Did they travel anywhere exciting?
- What advice can they give to you?
- What is their favourite memory of all time?
- Treasured family recipes

WRITE IT DOWN

Make sure you all spend a bit of time writing these stories down as a family, throwing in your own stories along the way. Copy photos and print them out. Or if photos are not available, have a go at sketching people – that can provide much amusement! Pop it all in a sketchbook or a notepad covered with fancy paper and keep it safe.

As we get older, it's important to know where we come from and to understand and appreciate our background. Maybe you will even solve the mystery of why Great Aunt Norma isn't talking to Cousin Tabitha. Or why Uncle Mo had one leg shorter than the other. Who knows what you will uncover!

CREATE A FAMILY TREE

Now that you are armed with lots of information about who is who in your family, why not create your own family tree? This is a simple way for youngsters to understand who comes from which side of the family and maybe they might even identify a few family traits that have been passed down, as well as a few physical resemblances!

CLEAR AND CLOUDLESS SKY?

If the time and weather allow, encourage relatives and friends to take you on a tour of their home town or village, pointing out all the unusual and interesting landmarks.

These memories stay with us. I can still remember the village where my grandfather planted an apple pip as a young boy and how the tree hung over the wall with its fallen shadow on the pavement as I walked underneath as a child, fascinated that my grandfather was once my age.

NOKEDLI PASTA

This is one of my favourite recipes. It was given to me by an elderly friend who as a child grew up in the most basic of conditions in Hungary, yet her life was filled with simple pleasures: this easy traditional nokedli noodles recipe for starters.

We use this as pasta and add our favourite sauce to it, along with any chopped veg we have in the house. It is so satisfying making your own pasta from scratch and brilliant fun for the whole family – if not a bit messy which always seems to go down well!

SERVES 4–6

Ingredients

- 500g (4 cups) plain flour (although '00' grade flour makes for a smoother pasta)
- 4 free range eggs
- 1 tsp salt
- 200ml (1 cup) water
- Olive oil
- Pinch of salt

Directions

1. Half fill your largest pan with water, a pinch of salt and drop of olive oil and put on the hob to boil.

2. Meanwhile, place the flour in a bowl and crack the eggs on top. Sprinkle the salt over the eggs, add the water and mix well to a gloopy consistency. Add a little more water if needed.

3. Once the pan is boiling, turn down the heat to medium. Holding a metal colander above the pan in one hand, ladle your dough into the colander, allowing the dough to drip through the holes into the water below, creating the pasta. Use the back of the ladle to help push it through if needed.

4. Gently stir through to separate the chunks. Allow to cook for a minute and when all the pasta has floated to the top, remove from the heat, drain and add a splash of olive oil to stop the pasta sticking.

If you have enjoyed making your own pasta, a nokedli grater instead of a colander makes light work of this. It is an inexpensive but worthy addition to your kitchen. It sits safely on top of the pan and allows you to 'grate' the dough into small pasta/noodle pieces, making it even easier.

Get Growing

This is not only a fun and fruitful activity for the whole family but will set your children up with the knowledge of where food comes from and how they can grow their own. With this in mind, start with growing food they enjoy.

INGREDIENTS FOR A MEMORABLE DAY
• Wellies • Old clothes so you can get stuck in • Seeds • Reuse old plastic boxes for mini greenhouses • Pots and containers • Soil or home-made compost • Watering can • Trowel and markers

---

CHOOSE WISELY
Only grow veg that is easy to maintain, unless you don't mind taking on watering duty when youngsters are not particularly bothered about getting involved (and there will be days).

Think about a whole meal that your family can cook from scratch together from only a quick trip to the garden – grow cherry tomatoes, spring onions, basil and spinach, all of which will be cropping at the same time, for a tomato sauce for pasta.

If you are planning on growing over the whole year, grow potatoes, butternut squash and white onions to make your own soup. You should be able to crop at the same time, or simply store your onions and potatoes if your butternut needs a little longer on the vine.

EASY STARTERS
Remember to label everything, as it won't be obvious for a while what everything is!
I recommend any of the following as being child friendly to grow and eat:

- Cherry tomatoes – pasta sauce (see recipe on page 106), salads, pizzas
- Large tomatoes – as above but fun to compete to grow the largest!
- Cut-and-come-again lettuce – make a simple salad with dressing and grated cheese
- Kohl rabi – resembles a spaceship and is great for stir fries
- Courgettes – perfect for making brownies (see recipe on page 65)
- French dwarf beans or runner beans – brilliant for little hands to pick
- Peas – they are perfect straight from the pod
- Mint – for minty pesto (recipe on page 73) and roast potatoes
- Potatoes – such fun to crop and for making crisps (see recipe on page 35)
- Basil – for pasta sauces and pesto
- Raspberries and strawberries – perfect for pudding and refreshing drinks
  (see sun water recipe on page 79 and raspberry fizz recipe on page 133)
- Chives – fab on everything, the flowers too are delicious and oh so pretty
- Radish – super simple and brightly coloured, but quite peppery for young ones
- Spring onions – a delicate flavouring for dishes
- Herbs – in fact, just have a full-on herb garden, great for little hands to pick

USE WHAT YOU HAVE

There's usually no need to buy new pots; just use what you have at home.

When starting your seeds, simply roll newspaper around a glass and flatten the base to make compostable pots that you can plant straight out. Reuse any old clear plastic boxes with clear lids as makeshift greenhouses to give your seedlings a head start. Cut the top and bottom off large clear plastic bottles to make great cloches. Egg cartons are perfect for chitting your potatoes.

When the plants are ready to be transported out to their new home, consider what you already have for pots. You can use old tyres, paddling pools, baskets, boxes, drawers, bins, buckets, crates, trugs, cans and even old wellies. Just remember to drill holes in the base (not in your new wellies of course). If you have any scrap wood, perhaps try building a box to line with a compost bag.

WATERING AND CROPPING

A word on watering – most plants don't like their leaves watered and this can often cause disease, so teach your youngsters to water just the roots. Have a set time each day, perhaps after school, to check if the soil is dry and whether they need a drop of water.

When the time comes, arm the youngsters with a colander or basket to head out and crop. If you're worried about overzealous hands pulling the whole plant out of the ground, let them use a small pair of scissors to snip off the crop, such as beans and tomatoes. Then get them making dinner!

NO GARDEN?

You need not miss out if you don't have an outdoor space; a windowsill is all you need. Here you can have a regular crop of cress on the go to throw in salads and sandwiches. You can also grow herbs on the windowsill – a long, skinny planter will fit in all your favourites.

If you have a front door outside, hang a bracket and a hanging basket, grow tumbling cherry tomatoes, basil and spring onions, and you will have a pasta dish sorted at least!

CREAMY TOMATO PASTA

Nothing beats a tomato pasta sauce from scratch, and this is a simple dish for youngsters to follow with a little help. We love this recipe, and somehow it tastes even better with the tomatoes freshly picked from the back garden. Young ones will be very proud that they have made something so fancy from their efforts in the garden.

SERVES 4

Ingredients

- 200g (2 cups) dried penne pasta
- 1 shallot or small onion
- 1 tbsp of butter
- 6 whole tomatoes or 500g (18oz) cherry tomatoes
- ½ tbsp balsamic vinegar
- Olive oil
- ¼ tsp salt
- 1 tsp sugar
- Small bunch of fresh basil
- 3 tbsp of single cream

Directions

1. Pop a pot of water on the stove for boiling the pasta, and when ready, cook the pasta as per the packet instructions.
2. Finely chop the shallot or small onion and fry in the butter until soft.
3. Chop the tomatoes and add them to the pan with the onion. Cover and cook on a low heat for 5 minutes until the tomatoes have softened.
4. Remove from the heat and mix in a glug of olive oil, the balsamic vinegar, sugar and salt.
5. Blend the sauce until smooth. A hand-held blender is great for this.
6. Chop up the basil and mix into the tomato sauce, along with the cream. Spoon over the cooked pasta.

Serve with a little grated cheese and a sprig of basil on top, together with a slice of crusty bread on the side and dig in!

World Cuisine

If you don't already mix up your meals, spending a month or two exploring different foods from around our wonderfully varied globe is most rewarding. I guarantee you will find one or two new favourites to add to your weekly repertoire in the kitchen.

INGREDIENTS FOR A MEMORABLE DAY
• Paper and card for passports and flags • Paint and some potatoes for making stamps • Books or internet for research • Ingredients for your chosen dish

---

TRY SOMETHING NEW

Be brave and look all around for inspiration. Try closing your eyes and pointing to a spot on an atlas to decide your next culinary destination. Don't be afraid to try new ingredients. You will find that many you have not heard of are surprisingly versatile and easy to add to your existing recipes. Wherever you 'visit', go as a family and get in the kitchen together.

AROUND THE WORLD

Make your own list or, if stuck, here are a few ideas:

- Nachos from Spain
- Pizza from Italy
- Vegetable sushi rolls from Japan
- Stir-fry noodles from Malaysia
- Lentil soup from Morocco
- Falafel wraps from Egypt
- Pad Thai from Thailand
- Ramen from China
- Nokedli from Hungary (see recipe on page 101)
- Spiced rice from Indonesia
- Tacos from Mexico
- Croque monsieur or croque madame from France
- Mild curry from India
- Moussaka from Greece
- Dahl from Ethiopia
- Burger and fries from America
- Maple syrup pancakes from Canada
- Marzipan fruit from Germany
- Baklava from Turkey
- Waffles from Belgium

> If you have friends and family who were born or grew up in a different country to you, why not ask to try out one of their favourite recipes from that region.

CREATING YOUR LIST

Jot down countries that you have always wanted to travel to but have never visited and then look up ideas of typical cuisine you may experience there. Oh, the places you'll go.

Also, consider places where you have travelled to and try to recreate that mouth-watering dish that you feasted on all holiday. I'm still trying to reproduce the tomato fritters that we experienced in Santorini; they were incredible. As hard as I wish, though, I simply cannot replicate the glorious Greek sunshine.

MAKE IT FUN

Create passports from card or paper, ready to be potato-stamped as you tick off countries you experience. Learn a few facts each time you 'visit' a new country. Draw and pin their flag up where you eat and maybe even suggest everyone brings an interesting fact to the dinner table about that particular place.

CLEAR AND CLOUDLESS SKY?

I'll always be the first one to suggest cooking outside. A simple gas stove or a BBQ, a chiminea or a firepit is all you need. For further suggestions see page 26.

Record Your Adventures

Start keeping a record of your family adventures, whether that be in a handwritten journal, including doodles and notes, or daily accounts in a secret diary, or in a scrapbook with photos and memorabilia.

INGREDIENTS FOR A MEMORABLE DAY
• Shoebox or large envelope to collect items • Notepad or folder • Plain and patterned paper • Photos • Keepsakes

---

KEEP MEMORIES ALIVE

This is a good way to encourage your youngsters to make memories of their own. The process of recording consolidates the memories you have made together.

I have always kept photo albums and am so glad I did. I like to recall fun times and see what a full life we lead. What the house used to look like, the garden too, crikey, us as well. What? There was a time before frown lines? Seems to suspiciously coincide with marriage and parenthood. Anyway . . .

Since we became parents, I have created a scrapbook for every summer and festive season. They are not always anything fancy. One year was blissfully relaxing, when both our cars broke down so camping holidays were cancelled. We went and adopted two kittens, a budgie and a tortoise (naturally) and we were forced to stay local. It meant I had the time to paint pictures for the scrapbook, write out inspirational quotes, accounts, print loads of photos and set it all out beautifully.

Another year, life was frantic, so I just printed all our photos, stuck them to sheets of fancy card and included lots of pictures drawn by our daughter, as well as any ticket stubs or brochures we had collected. It was messy. I love both of these scrapbooks equally, because both reflect what life was like that summer.

WHAT TO INCLUDE

Include anything you like, but here are a few ideas in case you get stuck:
• Photos and polaroids
• Quotes and reminders, goals for the future
• Notes about your day or the place visited
• Brochures and leaflets collected
• Children's artwork – drawings, paintings, scribbles, family portraits
• Your artwork (we took our watercolours everywhere one summer)
• Tickets and maps, keepsakes like sea glass and shells, pressed flowers
• Recipes of that season (one summer was literally wall-to-wall arancini)
• Lists – favourite tunes, places, foods, wildlife seen
• Create an A–Z for each family member

SETTING UP

You can start with a simple notepad. You can always jazz it up later! You may find that you are collecting quite a few mementos and photos, so you may need to upgrade to either a dedicated scrapbook or a ring binder or even a lever-arch folder!

You don't have to dress it up, but if you choose to there are lots of quick and easy ways to do this. You can add fancy lettering with stickers. Use pretty paper as pages. Create watercolour washes on plain paper to stick your photos on to. Allow your kids to go crazy with decorating if you like.

I like to number the days, for example a countdown to Christmas or Day One of the school holiday. Use calligraphy for quotes. Add cut-outs and stickers pertinent to your day – going to the beach? Get the youngsters to add sea life stickers. Coordinate your background artwork to the colours in your pictures. Spent the day in the garden? Paint the background green! Did you all have purple hair one week? Paint the background purple! Get the whole family involved to make it special.

COMPLETE IT

This is the important bit – complete your keepsake book. One September, school was mad, work was frantic, home life was beyond busy, blah, blah, blah. This meant we have a gap in our summer scrapbooks. And that makes me sad. But the truth is, you lose momentum once holidays are over.

Therefore, it's worth making a little effort. I like to be organized and keep it simple. At the beginning of the season, I grab an old shoebox and at the end of each day, I pop everything in – leaflets, tickets, collected leaves, whatever. I make a note of the date and what we did. When the day comes to compile everything I have all my bits and pieces to hand.

This is especially important for the festive season. It is now a joyful tradition that on the last day of the holiday, I print our photos and complete the scrapbook as, let's face it, once the decorations are down, we're on to pastures new.

CLEAR AND CLOUDLESS SKY?
You can create your scrapbook anywhere. In fact, my favourite one was compiled entirely outdoors because the summer just kept on going.

We were able to spend time painting the backgrounds in the glorious sunshine and they dried almost instantly, it was such a lovely end to the holiday.

Hello Holidays

YOU ONLY LIVE ONCE
BUT IF YOU DO IT RIGHT
ONCE IS ENOUGH

Get Crafty

We are a crafting family. We tend not to be the messy paints out, tape and glue all over the table and glitter everywhere types. Glitter was banned years ago after the floorboards sparkled for an eternity after a small-child-related mishap – it was very pretty though. Although creative messy sessions are important for expression, they don't always appeal to every member of the household. We like crafting projects where we can all get involved together, creating usable keepsakes which won't end up in the refuse bin after a few weeks.

INGREDIENTS FOR A MEMORABLE DAY
• Chosen craft supplies • Space to accommodate you all, such as a clear dining table
• Background music • Snacks and drinks

COLLECTIVE CRAFTING

Try to consider crafts that can be enjoyed by all – jam jar lanterns, woven wreaths from sprigs of rosemary, jewellery and candle making for gifts. The winter months are perfect for gift making.

We enjoy afternoons where we all gather around the dining table and place a large chunk of clay in the middle, each creating whatever we fancy – sculpture, tea light holders, leaf printed bowls. Sometimes, we even invite friends and family over for a session, making it more sociable and fun.

I do tend to hoard bits and bobs, making collections of random items in the attic. One such box contains nothing but corks. One day, I got busy making a linear corkboard on a skinny plank of wood with the wine corks. Meanwhile, our daughter sifted out the discarded bubbly corks (I'm really showing our true colours here) and made them into a family of penguins. Saving items for a later date allows you to repurpose them into bigger projects.

CREATE A PERMANENT FEATURE

A feature wall in blackboard paint or a ginormous wooden chalkboard made of ply is a great craft project that keeps on giving. Take it in turns to then create a mural on the chalkboard each week – such as a seasonal landscape or some inspiring words.

Our weekday planner is used constantly and is now a vital piece of organizational equipment in our home. Chalk is stored at the top so it's always available for anyone to write plans on the board.

TAILOR YOUR PROJECTS

Harry Potter has been part of our family for what feels like our daughter's entire life. She has been obsessed since she was three. Therefore, we tailor a few crafts to her interests – signage for the Leaky Cauldron which she can hang in a den or the treehouse, or magic wands from Ollivanders, made from chop sticks, hot glue and then spray painted.

Whatever the inspiration, encourage your family to come up with ideas: you will soon see that glitter need not be the staple of a memorable crafting session.

RELAX

Being creative does not come easily to everyone, and certainly not just because it is a designated afternoon, regardless of whether you have planned it in.

If you have older children that are simply not in the mood, don't force it. However, do encourage them to find an alternate activity that can be done with you, so at least you are still all together and able to chat and catch up. That, after all, is the most important factor here, being together and making memories.

CLEAR AND CLOUDLESS SKY?

Woodwork is a great outdoor activity, whether that is whittling a spoon or building and weatherproofing your new outdoor seating area. Get everyone involved – whittle around the firepit or give everyone a paintbrush to varnish the wooden frame.

Fingers crossed the weather will be gorgeous and you can all sit out later that evening toasting your hard work.

this week...

mon Bird watching

tue Olympics

wed Painting in the garden

thu Crumble making

Firepit

THE LEAKY CAULDRON

Camp in the Garden

It's always an exciting day when we dive into the attic gleefully to find the tent – although sometimes without the tent poles (don't ask). If you have all the required items to erect your tent, you can guarantee a cheerful day.

Firstly, who doesn't love squeezing a family, and a dog, into a two-person tent? Cosy doesn't cut it. If, however, you have an appropriately sized tent to accommodate the entire family, well, it's game on.

INGREDIENTS FOR A MEMORABLE DAY
- Tent (with poles) • Rugs, blankets, cushions • Duvets and pillows • Lanterns
- Low tables and chairs • Torches • Books, games and art materials
- Hot water bottles

SETTING UP
Make a day of it. Drag out your rugs, duvets, blankets and cushions. Set up low tables and seating. Gather your lanterns for later in the evening and get to work making it cosy. Spend the day outside with books, art materials, crafting projects, magazines, games. Make the most of the dry weather (fingers crossed) and all of that lovely fresh air (trust me, if you are all squeezing into that two-person tent, you will be thankful for the fresh air to knock you out later).

FOOD IDEAS
Try to plan a meal that can be made outside, whether that's a fry up on the gas stove, a BBQ in the sunshine, or even just something that is fun to make outside such as minty pesto – seriously, we cannot get enough (see recipe on page 73).

Think crumpets on the open fire. Maybe a flask of hot chocolate before bed. Maybe not. No wriggling child needs sugar before bed. Sandwiches are always fun when packed up on a tray for later. A picnic would be very civilized – with wine perhaps if you need a little courage to cram into that tiny tent. Those of you with a garden big enough to fit your ten-person tent, you're laughing.

EARLY EVENING
As the sun starts to set, light your lanterns and string some lights above and have a reading night until the bats come out to play. Play cards or Hangman or charades by candlelight.

Or have a star-gazing night with the lights out (see page 37 for ideas). First one to spot a star gets out of taking the tent down the following day (or keep it up for a few days

for extra fun – just be mindful of your grass yellowing). Or light a campfire in your firepit before bed. There's nothing quite like hypnotizing flames to put you in the mood for camping.

LATE EVENING

Remember your hats to keep you warm into the evening – and your hot water bottles – very important. Make sure everyone knows where the back-door key is for toilet trips and have one or two torches nearby if it is a moonless night. Explain to your cats that you're not in the mood for any 'live' treats this evening, nor any chilling fights with the cat next door. What jokers.

OVERCAST?
Camp in the lounge. Obviously. Lights out. Obviously.
No cheating and crawling off to your own beds at 2 a.m.

NATURAL INSECT REPELLANT

Spending so much time outdoors means you may be glad to have this home-made insect repellent to keep biting bugs at bay.

Shake before each use and dab a little bit on to your pulse points at the wrists, ankles and neck.

Grown-ups (unless you're clumsy) should be able to upturn the bottle to apply a small drop to the skin. A dropper bottle is even better. For youngsters, we find bamboo cotton buds are perfect for dabbing.

This repellant is made of completely natural ingredients but as with all essential oils do be careful the first time you use it. Just dab a little on the inside of your elbow and allow twenty-four hours to see if there is any reaction – hopefully not, but always worth checking.

MAKES APPROXIMATELY 50ML (¼ CUP)

Ingredients

- Rosemary oil
- Citronella oil
- Lemongrass oil
- Almond oil
- Small bottle or jar with a tight-fitting lid

Directions

1. Find your container.
2. Using the almond oil as a base, add 2 tbsp into a small pouring jug or straight into your receptacle if the opening is wide enough.
3. Next, add 8 drops each of the rosemary and citronella oils. Then 12 drops of lemongrass oil.
4. Pour the mixture in and close your bottle and shake vigorously to combine.

Jamming Session

Having a mini music session can feel quite primal and instinctive. It probably won't blend at first while everyone finds their footing. Fear not if there is a not a musical note within you. There is always something to play. The triangle is an obvious choice, but a rattle shaker or the humble xylophone is equally forgiving. If in doubt, bang a drum – kidding! Don't ever give the drum to someone without rhythm.

INGREDIENTS FOR A MEMORABLE DAY
• Musical instruments – grabbed from the toy box, a simple pan from the kitchen, or other wonderfully tuneful home-made varieties

---

RAID THE RECYCLING BASKET

If you don't have your own instruments, simply make them. An empty (obviously a great excuse to finish it off) ice cream box and elastic bands make for an excellent guitar.

An upturned saucepan with a wooden spoon makes a marvellous drum provided your nerves can cope. Balloons stretched over empty cans are a little less intense on the ears.

Fill an empty toilet roll or kitchen roll tube with pasta, cover both ends with paper and shake. Thread bells on to a bracelet for younger members of the family. Even a set of keys makes for a bit of fun, if your recycling basket is a little low.

TAKE IT SERIOUSLY

Why not move a level up? If you don't already, consider taking up an instrument. The recorder is a good start. Maybe a simple kalimba? Or even the harmonica? You may be pleasantly surprised at how cheap you might be able to pick up a guitar or violin at a second-hand shop.

If your child has been learning something at school, let them take charge and teach it to you. Or start with something simple – 'Frère Jacques' or 'Old Macdonald' are nice and slow to ease people in and, usually, everyone knows the words or make up your own!

LEARN A TUNE AND PUT ON A SHOW

If you have the time and dedication, learn a song together and put on a show for family or friends. You may find that the person who didn't fancy having a jam is now the one suggesting you all have a quick practice session.

CHEAP THERAPY

Music has played an important role in the family life of our ancestors from every region of the world for millennia. Music is a great stress reliever (unless you are completely and utterly tone deaf, in which case apologies for suggesting this as a family activity, where you may be ridiculed until the end of time) and a great way to shake off a bad day.

Imagine early hunter/gatherers needing to de-stress after coming face to face with a sabre-tooth tiger – music and dance would have been the solution. It's the same today, except now we travel by car and need to put our phones on silent, and the sabre-tooth tiger is actually a work colleague.

CLEAR AND CLOUDLESS SKY?

Now, I'm not saying you should take your orchestral skills out into the garden as I wouldn't want to offend any neighbours. No, I'm not dissing your skills, merely that the volume might penetrate through glass windows. If you live in the middle of nowhere or your neighbours have hearing difficulties, rock out.

However, you can get creative outdoors. Challenge everyone to create an instrument using only items they find in your back garden or near the home, if you only have grass or no grass at all (grass flutes are awesome by the way). Vote by majority rule as to which is the most melodic creation.

Scavenger Hunt

Scavenger hunts can be as easy or as difficult as you like. They can be linked to a time of year, the obvious being an Easter egg hunt, or just do it for fun. We like to have a hunt just before the summer holidays, and include prizes like water balloons to be used in the coming weeks.

INGREDIENTS FOR A MEMORABLE DAY
• Shoebox, egg carton, baskets or buckets • Home-made crosswords and rhyming clues • Coloured card or foam and lolly sticks for hiding numbers
• Printouts for nature hunts

DON'T FORGET
If you're hiding items make a note of what is hidden where – there's always one unfound item and if you're anything like me, you will forget where you put it.

KEEP IT SIMPLE
To keep it really simple, all you need is an empty egg box, or a shoebox, basket or a bucket. Challenge yourselves to find as many beautiful items in your garden as you possibly can. Remind youngsters not to pick anything unless you know they can and it's safe too. If they fill the basket, that's an extra point. Or paint the bowls inside the egg carton a different colour and use this to collect items that match that colour.

MAKE IT ELABORATE
Or go big. Every Christmas I make a scavenger for my better half. He must complete a home-made crossword or word search to reveal clues to the next location. There he will find another note, or a rhyming riddle that he must complete before the next one. I will typically hide ten clues for him to find before he has to hunt for his main present.

   My dad used to do it for me and I like passing this silly tradition on. Sometimes, they are so time consuming that everyone gets involved in between courses over Christmas dinner.

TIME AND TIME AGAIN
In the picture opposite, there are the numbers 1–10 hidden in the scene. These were made with leftover foam or you can use thick coloured card to cut out the numbers and then stick them to lolly sticks. Trust me, this appeals to all age groups. And is a great one for youngsters learning their numbers.

This is such a simple game, but it has been used for years and years around our home and garden as you each take it in turns to hide the numbers in either one room or the whole house. Just make sure it's fair and you hide them at the appropriate eye height. Just a tiny part needs to be visible, but nobody said camouflage was out.

PRINT IT OUT

A great way to encourage youngsters (and maybe us too) to learn about the world around us is to print out a page of different tree leaves and either use it in your own garden or take it further afield to help identify local flora (or use pages 142–3 for a few leaves to find). The next time you go, maybe it could be a printout of common grasses or wildflowers (or use pages 56–7 for a few flowers to spot).

OVERCAST?

Take it indoors, in fact this is our number one activity for rainy days. Hide items around the home to find or make a list of items that you need for dinner and make a game out of a mundane job. Hide the pasta in a really odd location if you want a giggle.

Mini Olympics

A fun way to spend a day in the sunshine is to create Mount Olympus in your very own garden, and hope that the ancient gods are on your side. Complete the day with opening and closing ceremonies.

INGREDIENTS FOR A MEMORABLE DAY
- Torch and beacon for Olympic flame (cardboard, tissue paper and a bucket)
- Flags and banners • Salt dough award medals • Sporting equipment
- Paper and pen to keep scores • Sparklers

Obviously, the competitive shenanigans cannot begin until the Olympic beacon has been lit. We made our torch from cardboard and tissue paper (see opposite bottom right), carried it through the house and around the garden, passing it on to the next person. Playing 'We are the Champions' whilst doing so makes it extra ridiculous. Then pretend to light the beacon (a bucket stuffed with tissue paper flames) to ooohs and aaaahs.

LET THE GAMES BEGIN
Once the 'flame' burns bright, let the games commence. Here are a few ideas:
- Egg and spoon (obviously)
- Sack race
- Skittles
- Darts
- Quoits
- Garden archery
- Table tennis
- Swing ball
- Boules
- Skipping
- Hula hooping
- Book balancing whilst walking
- Badminton
- Bean bag throwing
- Football, provided you don't own a greenhouse
- Running, provided you have the room
- Three-legged race, provided you live near an A&E

Perhaps the youngsters might like to suggest games or tournaments that they play at their own school sports day. My old favourite is pushing a tennis ball down a pair of tights into each foot. Pop the tights on your head. The aim is to swing your head and try to knock over empty bottles with the balls!

If you have a chalkboard, make a note of the scores throughout the day. The youngsters can tot them up at the end to determine the winner. Maybe introduce a penalty for cheating!

MAKE IT MEMORABLE

An opening ceremony can include hanging flags, singing a family song, strutting around the garden waving banners. Whatever you choose to include, make it memorable!

I actually made these start and finish flags for our wedding, a space hopper race to be exact. Yet, year after year, they make an appearance, and are perfect for a mini Olympics. To make your own, simply cut out letters from a darker fabric (I used old sheets for these flags) and appliqué or straight-stitch the letters on to a cut up white sheet. I made eyelet holes too so that they are easy to hang.

AWARD CEREMONY

Keep a tally of scores and hold an award ceremony afterwards. We made star medals from salt dough earlier in the week, then painted them gold, in preparation for the big day. What an honour to receive one.

The closing ceremony can be a turn around the garden, a conga line maybe to 'Eye of the Tiger'. In the evening, light some sparklers to close the event, allowing the flame to be returned to the torch for another day. Celebrate with a glass of raspberry fizz (see opposite).

OVERCAST?

Take the Olympics indoors, but think board games. Keep the Olympic flame alive by playing epic rounds of chess, Connect Four, Jenga, Scrabble, Monopoly, even crack the Twister out.

Hold dinner in the Olympic village – hang some flags and prizes around the dining room, play victory music in the background. Live like a champion, it's all about mental attitude.

RASPBERRY FIZZ

I use half of the syrup to a litre (4 cups) of water; that way I can make two pitchers on a warm, sunny day. However, feel free to add more syrup to your preference. The syrup will last for a few days in the fridge until the sun comes out again. If I have any raspberry fizz left over, I simply pour it back into a screw-top bottle to keep it bubbly for the next day.

MAKES TWO PITCHERS

Ingredients

- 200g (1½ cups) raspberries
- 100g (½ cup) sugar
- 200ml (1 cup) water
- 2 tbsp lemon (optional)
- 1 litre fizzy water or tonic water (4 cups)

Directions

1. Place the raspberries, sugar and water, along with the lemon juice if you wish (it makes it taste a little more like lemonade, which my husband loves), into a pan over a medium heat. Stir continually, squashing the raspberries with a wooden spoon as you go, it's marvellously therapeutic.

2. Allow to heat through until it is just about to simmer, when all the sugar has been dissolved.

3. Remove from the heat and allow to cool for ten minutes.

4. Using a muslin cloth or sieve, strain the mixture into a jug, squeezing out all the juice (keep the raspberries though). Add this beautifully coloured syrup to a pitcher jug, along with the fizzy water or tonic water.

Do not throw away those raspberries! Pot them up and store them in the fridge for a couple of days. Or use them that evening, served with vanilla ice cream, or the next morning mixed into porridge – so, so good.

Photography Day

Spend an afternoon at home taking photos. Lend your youngsters a camera or your phone and have fun with it. You may wish to document your garden in full bloom, to later print into a bound book as a keepsake. You may want to document an entire birthday weekend from everybody's differing perspectives. Or simply just have a bit of fun with photography prompts.

INGREDIENTS FOR A MEMORABLE DAY
• Camera or camera phones • List of prompts • Albums and frames when you are ready to print

---

TEACH THEM THE BASICS

Golden rule – keep the strap round their necks at all times. Because, let's be honest here, they will drop the camera, it's going to happen. Teach them how to focus on something and how to steady themselves. I suggest elbows in tight and take the photo when breathing out.

When you feel they're ready and not going to bump the lens into a stone statue, introduce macro mode. For little eyes who seemingly see everything, this is a wondrous affair, because now, it's REALLY close.

PHOTO PROMPTS

You can find lists of photographic prompts online, but here are a few to get you started, with optional subcategories to get your creative juices flowing:

- Nature – flowers, insects, trees, etc.
- Family – brother, mother, father, sister
- Emotions – happy, sad, doubtful, surprised
- Favourites – likes and dislikes
- Shadows – your own, leaves and petals, etc.
- Reflections – windows, mirrors, puddles, ponds, etc.
- Textures – smooth, hard, rough, shiny, etc.
- Colours – try to shoot the whole rainbow
- Height – tall versus short, small versus big
- Motion – tough to capture, but create stylized shots by creating your own motion; even moving the camera up and down in low light will get some great shots of sparks from an open fire
- Sleeping – cats, grandparent or other person, trees in winter
- Cosy – nests, burrows, dens
- Playful – bright colours, dancing, smiles, etc.

Or make your own set of prompts before you start, with everyone pitching in and each having to take one shot for each word. Compare notes afterwards and see how you all visualize things differently.

PRINT THEM OUT

Remember to print the pictures out if you can. But also remember to ask which their favourites are, not just yours. Our daughter knows her own mind and will relate a story as to why this picture of the robin is better than that one because, a second later, he flew at her, so that picture meant more to her than the one that was aesthetically pleasing to me. Nurture that expressionism.

If in doubt, print them all in black and white. Everything looks fabulous and poetic in black and white. Encourage them to name their works of art. 'Pink Flower' will do as a title, but this is an excellent opportunity to help them work with various adjectives, choosing the one they prefer. 'Delicate Jagged Petals' holds more emotion than 'Pink Flower'. See what they come up with.

DISPLAY THEM

If, like me, you have an old laminator kicking around with spare pouches, don't throw it in the landfill, adding to waste. Instead laminate a few of their favourite shots and use them as place mats, which will last a lifetime and make them feel so proud.

Alternatively, frame your favourites. I love the photo on page 134 of the hanging baskets for two reasons, it's stunning and it's from our daughter's perspective. Only a child would think to crawl under them to get the shot. Blow up your favourite photo and pop it in a frame and make an arty photographic statement in your hallway for guests to admire.

OVERCAST?

Spending the day inside with a camera is not necessarily a bad move, as it will encourage you to get more creative with objects and arrangements that you see every day and may not even truly see anymore.

Engage your abstract brain and encourage your family to do the same. Consider what you can use as metaphors. Outside, the prompt 'time' might have you chasing shadows, searching for a dried leaf or capturing moving animals, for example. However, inside, maybe you could look for a close-up of cracks in the ceiling to show the test of time or the toothpaste tube representing morning time. There is no wrong interpretation as we all view the world differently.

Nature Art

You need not venture out to buy supplies or purchase any equipment for this family art collaboration. All you need is your imagination. Have a rummage next time you are in the garden and all kinds of things will jump out at you as a possibility for an awaiting art project.

INGREDIENTS FOR A MEMORABLE DAY
- Natural objects from your garden or from your surrounding area • Your imagination
- A camera or camera phone to document your pieces • Wire, glue or string for more permanent projects

---

SEARCH FOR TREASURE

You will be surprised what you can find in your own backyard. Believe it or not, we often find prehistoric fossils in our gravel. And when I was kid, I was having a little dig in the compost at the bottom of the garden and unearthed a large fossilized sea urchin; I still have it to this day.

Of course, I'm not promising that you will find fossils on your first search; however, I'm sure most people will be able to find stones, leaves, seeds and sticks.

If you're anything like us, there will always be a collection of shells from previous trips to the beach and conkers from the autumn walks. Put them to good use and make pictures or sculptures.

MAKE ART

Check out artist Andy Goldsworthy for a little inspiration – he uses only natural objects to create wonderfully creative scenes.

Piled rocks are fun to make and look serene, stacked on display. No judgement, should you choose to use a little superglue. I admit, I most certainly did.

Try creating patterns or landscapes or choosing a word or phrase and encourage everybody to create something that they feel reflects that word or phrase, such as 'summer' or 'light in the dark'.

Your art need not be permanent. Although be sure to take photos and then put all the natural components aside to be used again.

GLUE AND STICK

Collect an array of tactile materials and challenge everyone in the family to create a scene on paper, a natural mixed media. Tailor it to your family's interests: do you have a budding fashionista in your realm? Challenge them to design a new outfit made entirely from leaves. Is there an architect? Challenge them to build an eco savvy home on a miniature scale.

WREATH MAKING

This version of art perhaps lasts a little longer. Collect skinny, softwood sticks like willow branches and bend them round into a circle, securing with wire or string. Now add your found treasures to keep the magic alive a little while longer. Have everyone add their favourite find of the day and hang it on your front door or garden gate.

OVERCAST?

You might need to plan ahead if the weather is not on your side. Simply collect items the day or morning beforehand and take it indoors. When playing with loose leaves, we actually prefer to find a sheltered spot or transport them to the dining table, purely so that the wind does not blow our artwork away before it is even finished!

Identifying Leaves

HAWTHORN *Crataegus*
Reputed to be the home of fairy folk. Hawthorn has a long history of being associated with magic and is believed to symbolize love and protection in Celtic mythology. Also known as the May tree because it blossoms in May. In a high breeze the falling blossoms look just like snow.

ASH *Fraxinus*
Referring to its leaves appearing in spring, my grandfather always used to maintain the summer weather could be predicted by 'oak before ash and we're in for a splash, but ash before oak, then we're in for a soak.'

BEECH *Fagus*
Personally, I believe beech trees provide the perfect dappled sunlight in summer. I also like their stubbornness, holding on to their leaves long after they have turned copper coloured, only to let them drop as the new buds push them off in the spring.

OAK *Quercus*
Often associated with the gods in various cultures, the oak symbolizes strength, knowledge and wisdom. It is always inspiring to think how tall and mighty the oak tree grows from such a small acorn.

MAPLE *Acer*

Always a treat to catch a glimpse of a maple seed spinning to the ground. Maples can live to be hundreds of years old. It is a lovely thought to imagine all those generations before us witnessing their autumnal rite of passage, as the leaves turn crimson before they fall.

HOLLY *Ilex*

Folklore suggests that if your holly tree is laden with berries, then we're in for a cold winter. The holly is synonymous with Christmas given its evergreen status. Once the decorations are taken down, our family always keep a sprig of the holly we brought in, as good luck for the next year.

HORSE CHESTNUT *Aesculus hippocastanum*

Always a sight for sore eyes in the school playground, conkers is a game that continues to thrill. Conkers are supposed to ward off spiders, but I once found a spider sitting on one, so maybe that is not entirely true.

IVY *Hedera helix*

Another evergreen keeping the colour going in the garden throughout the long winter months. Misunderstood and given a bad reputation, ivy actually provides safety and food for an abundance of wildlife.

Outdoor Cinema

This is one of my absolute favourite ways to spend an evening, whether it's late April, bundled up with blankets, at the height of summer when it's still ridiculously light out in the evening or during balmy September nights, as a last-ditch attempt to hang on to those hazy days. Side note – cinema evenings are best in the spring and late summer to ensure the evenings are dark enough to see the projection – not that it bothers me, but the family moans if it's too light.

INGREDIENTS FOR A MEMORABLE DAY
• Projector • White flat sheet • Net curtain wire to string it up • Screws or eye hooks to hold in place • Lanterns • Cushions • Blankets • Chairs, mats and/or beanbags • Movie of your choice • Popcorn • Milkshakes

---

A FEW WORDS ON PROJECTORS

An outdoor cinema needs less to set up than you might think. Sure, you can invest in a fancy projector, but an inexpensive, smaller version works wonders. In fact, for the same price as a family of four visiting the cinema, you can afford a projector for unlimited viewings. For years we used a projector found in a charity shop. When the laptop that we played it through broke, so did my heart. I love our outdoor cinema nights!

Since then, we purchased a much smaller projector that is a bit more modern and allows you to play from a phone, a TV stick, a DVD, you name it. The purchase was worth it for our family as we also like to build dens (you noticed?) and curl up inside before bed to watch something funny. We also love to take our little caravan away, and on rainy days, with all the curtains closed, the projector comes into its own. Take some time to consider whether the investment is worth it for your family. If not, borrow from a friend!

SETTING UP

What you see here is four eye hooks screwed into our wooden posts and a flat sheet strung up between. I turned over a small flap at the top and bottom and sewed to create an open-ended tube. With the use of two pieces of net curtain wire (cheap as chips) strung through the folds, it hooks on to the eye hooks nicely, stretching out the sheet.

Before we built the deck, we used another old white sheet, but with holes hemmed in each corner to keep them from fraying. We then fixed four screws into our outside wall and used them to display that evening's viewing.

All you need now are some chairs or beanbags, blankets and of course popcorn or make a quick batch of banana ice cream (recipe on page 159). Feet up. Press play.

USE CAUTION

Be careful what you watch if your neighbours can see into your garden! We were lent a movie, back in the day when we had just moved in and our shrubs were low. It was a comedy, but half way through, unexpectedly, one of the characters whipped his clothes off. Well, if the neighbours looked out their window at that moment, what a treat! Maybe that's why they moved shortly afterwards?

MAKE IT COSY

Wherever you set up, next to the house, under a tree, in a gazebo, on the lawn, make it cosy and warm for when the evening turns a little chilly. Bring out the blankets, the cushions, maybe the hot water bottles. Light the lanterns, bring it in close so that you can all snuggle up together, beanbags are perfect for outdoor cinema nights.

OVERCAST?

No, don't be put off by a little wind. Provided your speakers are good enough and don't annoy the neighbours, if your sheet is secure it makes it quite good fun – the character's faces billowing on the sheet can be very funny!

But obviously rain is a big no. If that's the case, think outside the box. We have made a nest in the lounge on the floor, making a massive bed out of duvets and pillows, laid down and watched a movie on the ceiling, before falling asleep on the floor. Or under the dining table if there's room. Kudos if you watch it from inside your tablecloth den (page 63)!

Miniature Worlds

Create a small world, such as a fairy garden or dinosaur park, in a corner of your garden and leave the youngsters to let their imaginations loose. Chances are, with a little help setting up, this activity will keep young minds inspired for hours – or even days. You can always add to the miniature world as you go along. Are pirates likely to attack? Fabulous, grab the washing up bowl, fill it with water and bury it in the sand pit to create one of the seven seas.

INGREDIENTS FOR A MEMORABLE DAY
• Selection of fairies, dolls, dinosaurs, cars, etc. • Collected natural items such as stones, shells, twigs, etc. • Items from inside the home such as string, baskets, scissors, etc.

MAGICAL KINGDOM

Our daughter has accrued a small collection of fairies from friends and relatives over the years. As soon as the weather brightens, we're outside, tidying up pots and planters, one of which usually becomes a miniature magical kingdom.

Using small cushions for comfort and a home-made bonfire for them to dance round, we create a small setting where they can raise unicorns, grow magical seeds and bottle potions. We use stones and shells collected from trips to the beach with a large, flat piece of slate being laid as the dancefloor, adding battery-operated twinkle lights once the sun starts to dip.

BEFORE TIME BEGAN

Alternatively create the land that time forgot and allow dinosaurs to roam free. Add stones, pebbles, shells, flowers, twigs, sand, whatever you have lying around and create a prehistoric scene. Dinosaurs don't need much, just a bit of undergrowth for the herbivores and maybe the odd small sacrificial dinosaur for the carnivores.

Create hides and caves from mud and leaves or upturned pots, small watering holes using a terracotta drip tray and soft bedding with chopped grass or hay. If you have the luxury of space, allow them to keep their garden up all year, maybe planting one or two small plants such as ferns or grasses to make it more realistic. And start practising your dinosaur roars.

STRETCH IT OUT

Why not stretch your miniature world across your garden? A piece of string and a small basket make for an excellent rudimentary cable car. Magical folk could take holidays adjacent to the pond or visit the treehouse of their ancestors or the beach in the sandpit. Maybe set up market stalls under the hedge and a theatre in the hollow of the tree trunk.

REIN IT IN

Or make it really teeny tiny and see how small you can make all the adornments for a miniature garden in case you ever get shrunk. Think about what would be most useful if you had to spend a day the same size as an ant. Maybe an acorn cup to catch water or tiny shells as plates. A toothpick as a spear for protection and maybe a rose petal hammock for a scented snooze.

OVERCAST?

If it's not nice enough to play outside, simply bring it in. Now's your chance to make a mouse house (page 66) or a little cottage. We often get out the folding tray and set up a two-storey scene – banquet on top, disco below. Obviously.

However, you could create a natural dining area with pebbles, bark and leaves on top and feathered beds in match boxes below. Dig out the battery-powered lights again for a little bit of magic.

Get in the Kitchen

I'm a huge fan of encouraging youngsters in the kitchen at every opportunity. Not only does it lay the groundwork for one of the most useful life lessons, it also helps them to see where food comes from and how it all comes together to make a dish. As well as getting them in the kitchen for baking sweet treats, get them in there with you for the savoury too. Although making a weekend pudding together every Friday is a fond ritual.

INGREDIENTS FOR A MEMORABLE DAY
- Ingredients for your chosen dish • Steps or low stool for younger ones
- Recipe books or your imagination

LEARNING THE BASICS

Start with easy things and work your way up. Breads are good – moulded bears and hedgehogs are brilliant for little ones. Pizza is the next step. Soups are easy. Ramen is simple. Chunky salads allow each person to prep one item – grate the cheese, drain the olives, slice the cucumber, drain and fry the chickpeas, for example. Nokedli is super fun to make (see recipe on page 101). Helping to tidy up afterwards is part of it all.

Savoury muffins are quick, and easy to eat for small hands (see cheese and tomato muffins recipe overleaf). Cheese scones are good. Gnocchi is exciting from scratch and very satisfying. Anything that involves using your hands to mix or mould or flatten or pat or roll is perfect for youngsters to really feel involved. It's not just youngsters that enjoy the making, I also like playing with my food so to speak, but most importantly, it's that time together in the kitchen.

EASY JOBS

Think safety first of course, but with proper guidance soft fruit and veg can be cut with a small knife or a child's safety knife depending upon age. Grating and peeling are excellent jobs to occupy young minds. I view the obligatory peeling of a knuckle as a rite of passage. In my experience, they learn and don't tend to get as close next time. We've all been there.

Mixing and stirring are very important duties. For these jobs it may be useful to have a small step handy nearby. Our kitchen steps make up an extra perch in our teeny, tiny kitchen, often being dragged around for my helper to get involved.

LET THEM CHOOSE

Ideally, when you have a little more time, a weekend perhaps, look through your cookbooks (or theirs) or borrow one from the library and allow your youngsters to choose a meal to assist with. Giving them ownership means the world to them and you may end up finding your new go-to. Maybe even make it their recipe; our daughter always knows she's up when pesto is on the menu (see page 73 for a recipe perfect for little hands).

OLDER CHILDREN TOO

I'm talking teens, maybe the odd twenty-something still at home who only ventures to the kitchen for pre-made snacks. Or maybe they don't even know the way to the kitchen. Hey, it happens.

   Ask them to plan a whole meal and, if competent, make the entire thing from scratch without aid. Linger nearby just in case but allowing a little bit of freedom in the kitchen can be liberating; you might even inspire a new hobby.

CLEAR AND CLOUDLESS SKY?

Baking can be tough outdoors, unless you are lucky enough to own an outdoor pizza oven – then you are truly living the dream.

   However, anything that can be cooked on a stove top can be moved outside with a small electric hob or a gas stove. Remember though, safety first. See page 26 for ideas on cooking outside.

CHEESE AND TOMATO MUFFINS

These are so scrummy. I wouldn't judge you for eating the whole batch from the oven. If they do make it to the tin for the following day, congrats – you're doing better than us! These work well for picnics in the woods, a welcome snack at the beach after your toes have frozen stiff from paddling, and also popped into a lunch box for school or work the next day. However, they are best enjoyed fresh and warm from the oven.

MAKES 12

Ingredients

- 350g (2 cups) cherry tomatoes (or green tomatoes that have not ripened)
- 100ml (½ cup) milk
- 2 free range eggs
- 50g (½ stick) butter, softened
- 150g (1¼ cups) plain flour
- Pinch of salt
- 2 tsp of baking powder
- 150g (1½ cups) grated cheese
- Extra grated cheese and fresh chives for topping

Directions

1. Preheat the oven to 180°C/Fan 160°C/Gas 4/ 350°F
2. Finely chop the tomatoes and leave to one side.
3. Mix the milk, eggs, softened butter, salt, flour and baking powder until well combined.
4. Mix in the grated cheese and the chopped tomatoes.
5. Carefully spoon the mixture evenly into a greased muffin tin (silicone moulds are great for small hands to help pop them out later), filling each muffin cup to the top.
6. Sprinkle the tops with a little more grated cheese and a few chopped chives.
7. Bake in the oven for 25–30 minutes, until the tops start to brown.
8. Allow to cool on a wire rack for ten minutes. Now walk away, so that you won't be tempted until it's time to serve them. However, they are delicious warm. Just saying.

Put on a Show

Everyone has a talent, some questionable, others more genuine. Regardless, let them shine by putting on a show to the rest of the family. It could be a ballet, tap dance, rock gig, violin recital, magic tricks, opera, stand-up comedy or a nature show with special guests (thanks to our very own chickeroos).

Make a plan. Schedule your acts and allow a little time for everyone to be able to practise, and then practise a bit more. Never work with children and animals they say but, really, they make for the best shows!

INGREDIENTS FOR A MEMORABLE DAY
• A stage area • Seating or blankets and cushions • Paper, watercolours and pens for posters, schedule and tickets • Signage, for example 'Queue Here'
• Jug of water and glasses • Intermission snacks • After-show party food and drinks
• Optional lighting and props • Music

THE VENUE
You can set your show up anywhere; the lounge is always a winner as the seating is already arranged. However, outside works well if it's dry, providing a little more room as dance shows tend to spill off the stage, making it a more immersive experience.

Your stage can be anywhere and as elaborate or as simple as you like – a covered gazebo, in front of the flowerbed, on the lawn, at the park. As long as you leave enough room for your guests to be seated and maybe for a few refreshments.

SETTING UP
You have planned your stage, now set a time and date. Be sure to make posters, tickets and signage, encouraging everyone to get involved. Build a bit of anticipation by creating a mini trailer if you wish and send it to all the members of the audience, so they get a sneak preview of what is to come. Stick your posters up around the house a few days prior, or hours before.

On the day, prepare your stage. Are you adding curtains? Do you need a table and chair? Remember a glass of water, placed out for each act should they need it. Add lighting if required. Following tradition, perhaps have some flowers for the audience to throw at the performers once they are finished. Do you need music? Or any other props? Make sure it is all nearby.

Why not go all out with a garden circus? Get the bunting out and set up areas for balancing acts, plate spinning and hula hooping. Involve the family pets (safely of course) with their tricks.

Gather your seats from indoors, or folding camping chairs, or even keep it simple with blankets and cushions laid down on the floor for your audience. Pop your signage up. Allow your crowd to queue before handing in their tickets and let the show begin.

INTERMISSION

Why not have an intermission and serve banana ice cream to the audience? Try the recipe opposite, it's so simple and easy, not to mention delicious and a great way to use up soft bananas. Perhaps even get one of the elders to do a stand-up sketch in between sets, to keep the audience warm, or play music in the background.

AFTER-SHOW PARTY

Celebrate afterwards with a glass of raspberry fizz (recipe on page 133) and canapés or finger food for a bit of fun. Keep the music playing in the background, just be mindful of your neighbours.

OVERCAST?

Our favourite show was actually a Christmas pantomime, our daughter playing all the parts, with the dog, tortoise, budgie, chickens and cats all making cameos throughout. I recorded it and edited it into a short video. We emailed this to absent family with specific instructions to watch it at 3 p.m. on the following Saturday afternoon. We then had an after party via video conferencing.

Therefore, if it's a bit grotty outside, fear not as you can always take your show indoors and online to share with a wider audience.

BANANA ICE CREAM

This super simple ice cream from just one ingredient is pretty special as it is healthy and scrummy too. It is really important to use brown spotted bananas though, so save the banana bread for another day.

This is perfect on its own, or you can add chocolate sauce and sprinkle a few crushed nuts over the top (pecans and walnuts are delicious).

SERVES 1

Ingredients

- 1–2 ripe bananas per person

Directions

1. Chop your ripe bananas up into rounds; they need to be spotty or your ice cream won't be sweet and creamy.

2. Either lay the pieces out individually on a baking tray to freeze or keep them in a reusable bag or Tupperware pot in the freezer. Leave them overnight and use them within a month ideally.

3. A highspeed blender or processor works best. We have a superduper fruit sorbet maker from a charity shop, which works brilliantly and has no trouble with the frozen banana. If you are using a blender or a processor and it struggles to blend it up smoothly, try putting a fresh, unfrozen banana in first and then add the frozen pieces on top.

4. You should now have silky smooth banana ice cream ready to rock and roll.

Dine Differently

By now, you must have grasped how much our family love food. We eat outside as often as the weather allows. However, we don't just stop there. We like to mix it up, location and time of day, lunchtime picnics being a different beast to an evening BBQ, breakfast again different to afternoon tea. Dappled light versus setting sun? It's a difficult choice.

INGREDIENTS FOR A MEMORABLE DAY
- Your imagination and sense of adventure • Moveable chairs or washable blanket
- Essential items like cutlery and napkins • Jug of water or drinks bottles
- Your chosen meal or ingredients to make outside

THINK OUTSIDE THE BOX
You don't need to restrict yourself to mixing it up outside though; think about switching it up indoors too. I'm not saying move into the bathroom for bagels (although a cold glass of wine in a warm tub is not to be sniffed at, but how often does that happen once you become a parent?); however, use what you have and consider how it might be altered to accommodate your feast.

DINING IDEAS WE HAVE ENJOYED
- Continental breakfast picnic on the lawn, with a large blanket spread out for lounging
- Breakfast baguettes on the doorstep, soaking up the sun
- Full English on the gas camping stove with the chickens roaming free
- Pastries on the windowsill, welcoming the morning
- Packed lunch in the treehouse, after an adventure in the garden
- Open sandwiches in the hallway, keeping the door wide for a fresh breeze
- Take your ingredients out under a tree, like our pesto (see recipe on page 73)
- Make a den (ideas on page 81) and tray up a meze feast
- Spread out a picnic blanket on the bed and enjoy fresh bread and cheese
- Dine like royalty in the play shed, matching your meal to the play food you have
- Set up a cosy corner at the bottom of your garden for a new view (try not to make a mental job list of what needs cleaning from this perspective!)
- Turn your shed into a bar and enjoy snacks and aperitifs
- Pop up a gazebo or tent and string with lights and lanterns for a fancy three-course meal
- Gather around a firepit and cook dough sticks (page 97) and stew (page 31)
- Drag a table and chairs to the spot in your garden that gets the last of the sun and enjoy hotdogs as the sun goes down

TIME OF DAY

Having a picnic in the treehouse during the blazing sun, with the dappled light providing welcome and stunning shade, is very different to eating tacos up there for dinner, with the candles flickering and the garden festoons gently swaying in the breeze. Both feel like a new experience. So do not just stop at changing where you eat for one day; try what time of day to eat there too. Plus, the season will show you different secrets as you look up into the canopy.

TIPS FOR EATING ANYWHERE

Here are a few things I've found to help us move easily around the garden, usually with the sunshine. Folding chairs or low stools are brilliant. An upturned crate is our moveable go-to table. A dedicated blanket kept at child height, so you can announce the plans and give them a job to kick start the excitement. Outdoor cushions that transfer well to sitting on the ground are a must.

We keep a wooden tray of spare cutlery and napkins in a basket which our daughter fetches whenever we eat outdoors. Wooden bowls and chopping boards as plates are great for transferring outside, and unspillable drink bottles are a prerequisite. It's better not to be too precious about spillages though. Blankets and cushion covers can usually be cleaned. The amount of time I've said 'be careful' and then it ends up being me knocking something over!

CLEAR AND CLOUDLESS SKY?

Make the most of the seasons. Morning brunch in spring is a real treat in the sunshine, the height of summer brings many opportunities for shaking up your meal locations; however, autumnal firepits are cosy and lunch overlooking snow falling from a window seat, snuggled up in the warm, is magical.

Play Shop

Lazy weekends in the sunshine are simply glorious. They always seem so few and far between. When they do roll round occasionally, they are often interrupted by the young ones wanting to be entertained. And although it is so good just sitting in the sun – you had forgotten what it was like – how can you resist those little faces? My solution? Create a play shop, a farmer's market if you will. If they stock real iced coffee and cake, that's a bonus.

INGREDIENTS FOR A MEMORABLE DAY
• Custom-built play shop or low table • Table and chairs for the café • Play food and home-made ones too • Play money in a jar or till • Calculator • Chalkboard or whiteboard for signage • Garden umbrella for a little shade • Paper bags • Steps for shelves • Pen and paper for taking orders and making a price list

---

SETTING UP
It does not need to be anything fancy. Simply drag out a low table or set up at the end of an outdoor table. Our play shop is a sweet stand we made for our wedding, and then viciously chopped its legs off to make it child height. Usually, it lives in our play shed and masquerades in turn as a restaurant, a patisserie, a market stall, a spy headquarters and an ice cream parlour.

If you have any spare wood in the garage, or a spare pallet, then you can simply build a dedicated play shop with or without a stall back. This one was made from an old banister rail and a bit of ply for the counter, spare batons made up the edging and supports. If you have a play till, perfect. If not, we've found an old Nutella jar filled with play money works a treat. If you don't have any play money, make crayon rubbings of real coins on paper and cut them out to use.

WHAT TO SELL
Here are some ideas:
- Felt food – carrots, tomatoes, lettuce and cookies are easy to make with felt
- Salt dough bread loaves and plaited baguettes – store them inside so they don't go soggy though
- Recycled packets and boxes
- Wooden cheese tubs, empty milk bottles and egg cartons
- Silicone cupcake cases, filled with wadding, sewn shut with felt and decorated on top
- Play food you might already have
- Save any miniature bottles of wine you may receive as gifts
- A bottle of real wine maybe

- A few hardy vegetables from your own supplies
- Garden flowers and potted herbs
- Cookie-shaped beanbags – perfect for mini Olympics (page 130) or a garden fête (page 173)
- Real snacks to sell as part of the café section
- A jug of cold coffee or milkshake to be served over ice

LITTLE EXTRA TOUCHES

Bring out any paper bags saved from shopping; birthday box bags are always worth saving for just this sort of occasion and make perfect shopping bags. Put up your chalkboard or whiteboard signs saying that the shop is open and what exciting wares are on offer. Create a gardening section selling your watering can and trowel, packets of seeds. Use steps as shelves, they display merchandise beautifully.

Drag a small table and chair out for the café. Allow the youngsters to pick a few flowers to decorate their shop, maybe even pull the bunting out? Might as well. Create a price list and leave them a calculator to use. Let them arrange it how they like and shout out when they are open for business. In the meantime, you will be deliberating over the wine list.

To make your own play shopping bags, cut out rectangles of fabric, hem the shortest sides, fold in half and sew the two longest sides closed to make little reusable bags for play. Striped fabric looks really authentic.

SHOP BEFORE DINNER

Maybe even throw in the ingredients for your tea that night and go 'shopping' beforehand. Teach them to keep fresh goods in the shade so that they do not spoil. Perhaps even cook outside with a gas stove or over a firepit to truly make the most of the sunshine (ideas on page 26).

OVERCAST?

This is an easy one to take indoors, hassle free. Let them take over the coffee table or the dining table for the afternoon. Perhaps help your family to make real biscuits or cake to sell at the shop. Everybody wins.

You may even have a play kitchen that you could incorporate as part of the play, serving 'hot' meals throughout the day. Perhaps allow them to keep the freshly baked cakes (once cooled, of course) in the pretend oven to be served 'fresh'.

FRESH BREAD!

PRICES

FARM SHOP & CAFÉ

King or Queen for a Day

Allow youngsters (and why not include yourselves) to be king or queen for the whole day. Chocolate for breakfast? As you wish. Bedtime at midnight? So be it. This is a great activity for teaching decision-making and how to handle responsibility. The golden rule is that everyone must be able to take part.

INGREDIENTS FOR A MEMORABLE DAY
• Card for making a crown • Tablecloth or scarf for a cloak or cape • Imaginations

---

TEACHING RESPONSIBILITY

Allow them to create a plan for a whole day and see what they do with their powers. If it gets a little out of control, for example, the whole day eating chocolate, gently hint that maybe you will choose for everyone to eat snails when it's your turn. All day. I actually feel a little bit nauseous writing that down. I had a bad experience; they say time is a great healer.

If the question of money comes up – like they want to go shopping, for example – either set a small limit for a treat for everyone and allow them to manage the funds – is there enough for lunch out or just an ice cream for everyone? Alternatively, set the rule early in the day that it's a no spend day. And whilst we're discussing the basics, safety trumps royalty.

OUT OF THE BOX IDEAS

If anyone gets stuck, here are a few suggestions:
- Breakfast in bed
- Pyjamas all day
- Ball pond in the bath
- Watch a sunrise or sunset
- Choose everyone's outfit
- Hold a spontaneous party
- Forfeits when the king or queen is not listened to
- Sleeping in the lounge
- Late bedtimes and lazy mornings
- Breakfast for dinner and vice versa
- Spend the day in your finest outfits
- Get volunteering
- Create a crazy recipe from scratch and everyone must try a bit

MAKE IT LEGIT

You will need to hold a ceremony in the morning, the royal taking the pledge to do their best throughout the day, and there should definitely be some crown making going on. Cloaks too, I cannot wait for the day when cloaks and capes become cool for all.

TAKING CONTROL

If you have older youngsters at home who are most likely to choose sitting and watching TV all day, you have two choices. Go with it. Who said a day lounging is a bad thing? I actually dream of days like that. However, you might like to get a little more creative and give them the reins. When it's their turn, maybe make a few suggestions depending on their age, such as allowing them to choose the route of the dog walk and you will follow them anywhere. Perhaps they would like to plan and cook the meal for dinner. Would they like to capture the day on their camera phone and make a doccumentary about family life? Dangerous, I know. However, given a little freedom to allow them to test out their adulting brains, they may even surpass you. It's easily done in this house.

CLEAR AND CLOUDLESS SKY?

You could put a caveat in place that the whole day must be outside, so it really gets their creative juices flowing for what you can do either in the garden or the local neighbourhood.

If the sun's out, even better, but if not, maybe allow the plans to adjust throughout the day in case Hurricane Bernie hits at two in the afternoon, despite the cloudless sky all morning.

Garden Fête

Who doesn't love a village fête? The incredibly wobbly coconut shy, the local VIP shouting through the loudspeaker system, their voice getting raspier by the hour, the tug of war, where even the shyest of participants find their strength on the battlefield. However, British weather does not always play ball, and sadly, it's never quite the same in the rain.

A garden fête at home, however, can be planned on a kind weather weekend, and is a wonderful excuse to get family and friends over to join in too.

INGREDIENTS FOR A MEMORABLE DAY
• Bunting (obviously – see page 45 for a DIY) • Chalkboard • Microphone or recycling to make one • Cakes on cake stands • Patterned plates and teacups • Garden games • Small items for a lucky dip or raffle • Flowers for arranging

---

SETTING UP
We set up a fête area with stalls under cover and a playing field area on the grass for games. It would not have been complete without a microphone; however, to the relief of our neighbours, at the last minute, I decided to leave it unplugged – brilliant fun all the same.

Open the fête by cutting a ribbon to your garden. With an announcement, of course. You could set up a maypole for dancing round, the washing line with ribbons will do. Even encourage your family to possibly create a crazy dance inspired by traditional Morris dancing. Or not.

We had to have a raffle and lucky dip (constructed of items from the attic and leftovers from party bags), a cream tea with cakes, and a homegrown vegetable show (or simply using veg stolen from the fridge). If you have an extended feathered and furry family, a pet show is a must; naturally Dex won, because he was the only one who sat still for it. If you have no pets, drag the cuddlies out, although judging them might cause family arguments.

VILLAGE GAMES
With regards to the games, some ideas we have loved are tug-of-war (with hilarious consequences given the weight differences), quoits (made from wood and duct-taped rope), welly throwing (provided you have the space!) and splat the rat (a bit of drain pipe tied to a ladder with a board lent up behind, use a rounders bat to splat with – we randomly have a teddy rat from Father Christmas, not sure the big man had this in mind for him though).

Try your hand at croquet, badminton, build a coconut shy from old windbreak poles with tennis balls cut in half and screwed on top (pop the badminton net or old sheet behind to catch the balls). Discover the weird and wonderful world of egg rolling. Maybe give the smashed china a wide berth.

Beg, borrow and steal from friends and neighbours for supplies, why not invite them over to join in! Or tap up the charity shops for second-hand items to make it feel quaint and oh so English country garden.

ACTIVITIES

Get the family involved with making bunting for the big day. Make butterfly cakes and shortbread in advance, let the youngsters decide how to decorate them. It would probably be rude not to make a Victoria sandwich, perhaps even have a go at making your own jam for the filling and then 'sell' it at the fête. Make some cheese scones and ploughman lunches to fuel the fun. Pimm's tent? Could work. Who am I kidding, it always works!

Set up a crafts stall in the shade for some downtime and even a flower arranging table with blooms and foliage from your garden. Use old jam jars to create masterpieces. You could have a plant stall where you take cuttings of nearby parent plants and pot them up.

And then when you all need to relax after all the games and activities, set up the face painting table, allow the youngsters to do your faces, no excuses!

HAVE A LAUGH

Having regular announcements via the microphone is brilliant (or use a scrunched-up piece of foil taped to an empty kitchen roll tube). You might feel silly at first, but I can guarantee, you will all be racing for the mic by the end of the day.

As with all these activities, make it fun and have a giggle. It doesn't need to get (too) competitive and remember to involve everyone in the planning so that they feel invested in the day. But most of all, stay in the moment and take lots of photos. I wish you albums and albums full of fun.

OVERCAST?

If you need to move it inside, set up a different stall in each room and drape your bunting from room to room to bring it all together. Indoor games could include Pictionary, Five Second Rule or a legendary dance off.

Tea and cake are always welcome, whether indoors or out. Serve fruit tea for the youngsters and maybe have an ice cream stand in the corner to keep the sun shining inside, even if that simply entails a cool bag with ice packs working overtime.

best in show

lucky dip!

OE

lucky dip!

RAFFLE
TO BE DRAWN AT
3 PM

Acknowledgements

I would absolutely love to shout my thanks and love to a few people for making this happen. Please bear with me. I would firstly like to thank Matt Ralphs, for encouraging me to embrace my love of writing and to get these ideas down on to paper. If you do not already own any of his children's books, do check them out. He is an inspiration.

Secondly, I would like to thank all of the youngsters who have ever crossed our threshold for after-school fun through childminding. I always had an absolute blast with you all and our adventures together inspired the framework for this book. You guys rock.

Thirdly, my husband. Yeah, you can have a mention. You are wonderful, in many, many ways, but I will get told off for listing them all here and well, quite frankly, I am biased, so I will just say thank you for your unwavering support and for being my first playmate to adventure with.

Next, I would like to thank our very glamorous daughter, who is always up for fun, anytime, anywhere, whilst wearing clip-on earrings and an expertly styled outfit. She has the patience and wisdom of a human much older than her six years and constantly inspires me with her resilience, her love of the natural world and her enthusiasm for all things (especially food). Her constant cheer makes for a joyous day every day.

Also, thanks Fogies for cheering me on from afar. You started all this by setting me up right with a fun-packed childhood filled with our own adventures, steeped in nature, and for starting the notion of an extended furry and feathered family. You are where it all began.

A tremendous thank you to Anna Sanderson at Pimpernel Press (who happens to be an incredible artist too) for your belief in this book, for helping to make it a reality and your constant support throughout; it really has been an honour to work with such a fabulous publishing house. And, of course, thanks to everyone behind the scenes at Pimpernel Press for your hard work in translating this into a tangible object. You have all made a dream come true.

I would also like to thank Esther Parry (whom I share my birthday with!) for introducing me to the wonderful world of Hungarian cuisine, such as the nokedli featured in this book. Together, we are hoping to inspire the next generation to embrace cooking from scratch at home as it need not be complicated, as her simple and fun nokedli recipe demonstrates.

And finally, a heartfelt thank you to our camera, which survived (mild) falls and a missing lens cap on numerous occasions, you are a true companion constantly by my side. Speaking of which, I had best mention Dexter. That wonderful pooch who actually never leaves my side and, as you can probably tell, is ever present in all our adventures, making them all the more special. Also, a shout out to the rest of our photogenic feathered and furry family members – Poe, Archie, Boo, Angus, Logan and the fluffy bottomed ladies Gladys, Margaret, Elizabeth and Bertha.

Wishing everyone who reads this book, many, many happy adventures at home. Treasure every moment and take lots of photos, as before you know it, they'll be all grown up, asking to borrow your camera to document their own adventures. And so it goes.